# John Henry Goodwin
# Master Mariner *of* Liverpool
# Life At Sea (1865 – 1915)

First Published 2013 by Countyvise Ltd
14 Appin Road, Birkenhead, CH41 9HH

British Library Cataloguing in Publication Data.
A catalogue record for this book is available from the British Library.

ISBN 978 1 906823 80 1

# Contents

*Introduction*     *i*

*Acknowledgements*     *x*

| | | |
|---|---|---|
| 1. | 1850 Born in Liverpool | 1 |
| 2. | 1865 A Sailor's Life | 11 |
| 3. | 1874 Appointed Second Officer | 20 |
| 4. | 1881 Unexpected Arrival Home | 26 |
| 5. | 1884 New York | 32 |
| 6. | 1889 A Close Shave | 40 |
| 7. | 1890 The Coming of Steam | 50 |
| 8. | 1891 Pilgrims for Jeddah | 57 |
| 9. | 1894 Master of the Ajax | 71 |
| 10. | 1896 Bound for China | 84 |
| 11. | 1900 Australia | 95 |
| 12. | 1902 Maiden Voyage in the Telemachus | 110 |
| 13. | 1905 Liverpool | 124 |
| 14. | 1908 Reminiscences | 132 |
| 15. | 1908 Second Steward Lost | 156 |

16. 1909 Family Affairs                                        164

17. 1909 To Australia Again                                    169

18. 1910 A Survivor Found                                      173

19. 1910 Receives Award from Mayor                             178

20. 1911 Surprises at Dalny                                    188

21. 1911 Christmas                                             193

22. 1912 Meets the Devenishes at Kobe                          199

23. 1912 Twenty-Second Voyage in the Telemachus               204

24. 1913 A Child's View of Heaven                              208

25. 1913 Family Affairs                                        214

26. 1914 Chinese Burials                                       220

27. 1914 Outbreak of War                                       229

28. 1915 War Continues                                         237

29. 1915 Last Voyage                                           247

*As Seen By Others*

British Steamer Takes Immense Cargo                            257

"Ship Subsidy Will Not Do", Says Captain Goodwin               262

A Survivor Found At Sea                                        265

# Introduction

John Henry Goodwin was born in Birkenhead in 1850. He went to sea at 15 and shipped people and goods round the world for half a century until the age of 65. During this time he oversaw the transition from sailing ships to vast liners powered by steam, although it was his opinion to the end that real sailors only truly flourished under sailcloth. He began as an apprentice on a number of ships and ended up as Master of the steamship Telemachus, which had a hold capacity of an astonishing 12,000 tons. He personally witnessed some early scenes in the American Civil War as well as the opening of the Great War of 1914 – 1918, in which by luck he saw no action except that his ship was fitted with an artillery piece in the event of being discovered by German destroyers.

At some point in this long career he started writing down his memories of life at sea which he continued to update until his final voyage. On retirement in 1915 he passed his notes and chapters to his niece, Minnie Mitchell, who typed them up for him—197 pages of faded, yellowing foolscap. For almost a hundred years they stayed like that, still in his sailor's chest which passed down through the family, but have at last come into print as Life At Sea (1865 – 1915), the book which you have in your hands.

The early pages of the Life give a brief account of his birth and first experiences but in no time at all he is on to one of his favourite subjects, namely ghosts, giving us a glimpse of that Victorian world where ghosts push open bedroom doors at night or run up and down stairs or stand behind us in the cellar when we are fetching up coal. Strangely enough, this comes in handy many years later when he lands in Hong Kong, where he recounts a story of some Chinese who are fearful of entering their cabin on account of a ghost still occupying the bunk that he had been used to sleeping in in more corporeal days. The ghost also, rather annoyingly, insists on coming down and sitting with them at mealtimes. John's trusty Chief Officer, in full view of the Chinese, goes into the cabin one night, grabs the ghost, lures it along the deck and finally disposes of it overboard with one almighty boot. The Chinese pronounce themselves completely satisfied.

It is not long before the ambitious young man becomes second officer on the Baroda and not long after that, at 31, he is promoted to Master. This is the top of the hierarchy—to have Command, and Command is what he is after. After all, his own father had Command, and first took him on board from Liverpool to New York at the age of 11. It's not surprising in retrospect that he gave up working in the office of a cotton broker and followed his father in the great trade of the sea.

Much of Captain Goodwin's time is put to good use in making notes in his log (Captain's log, Steamship Telemachus, year 189–). He notes his position, his direction, the wind speed, longitude, latitude, the amount of water available, and whether that water is fresh water, dirty water treated with alum, or simply estuary water which the crew have to drink out of sheer desperation, crossing their fingers that they will not fall victim to cholera, malaria or plague. Some chapters simply record ports of departure, ports of arrival, with the dour observation that nothing much had happened on that voyage, a voyage that may well have lasted for three months. And yet, a while later, his imagination will suddenly seize upon an incident and off he goes again. He recalls being in Calcutta, for example, and coming across a 'Hindoo' burial ground. He is taking himself off for a walk to collect his thoughts when he stumbles across a compound filled with skulls and bones, and further on sees the 'Doom Wallahs', as he calls them, sitting around an open fire burning bodies of the deceased, prodding and poking them to make sure they are fully combusted.

Sailing then was a manly world and our Captain, John Goodwin, is not at all sure about the wisdom of having 'ladies' on board. He recalls a wonderful incident in the Bay of Biscay where two ladies are being thrown out of their bunks in the middle of a hurricane, and after attempting to settle them again, unsuccessfully, he resorts to lashing them to a stanchion, an upright post, so that while the ship may well be on the point of falling into the deep at least they won't hurt themselves on the way down. He has done his duty by his passengers, but it is easy to surmise that under his breath he is saying 'never again' to 'ladies'. He has the good grace to admit afterwards that he had never seen a ship roll like it before or since.

John Goodwin believes in God and Queen Victoria, Parliament some of the time, and as for Democracy—he approves of it, but especially when others vote his way. He is not with the radicals. He believes in a husband's duty to provide for his wife, and calls to mind his Australian nephew by marriage who he describes as 'utterly worthless, absolutely failing to provide for her (his niece)'. He believes in families staying together, in playing the long game, in seeing a completed life through. In passage after passage he thanks God for having a wife and home to go back to in Liverpool, and for God's having bestowed upon him the wife that he has.

As for the social issues of the day, especially the growing question of women, he remains stalwartly unperturbed. His wife he refers to as 'the little Mother', and leaves the reader in no doubt as to what he would do to Miss Pankhurst's bottom if he had her across his knees. If only he could have put Miss Pankhurst and her followers into a little box he would have done it and closed the lid. His 'feminist' relations in Australia fill him with grudging respect, however, an admiration verging on awe, as he gets the first inkling of the way the future is passing him by. He attends a meeting of the Australian National Women's League and comments that he was very much struck 'with the able speeches made by two of the ladies'. He is 'not only surprised, but delighted by what they said, and the way they said it', concluding lugubriously, 'they were both married ladies'. Seeing an aeroplane for the first time, in Sydney, he knows in his sailor's bones that aeroplanes aren't a good thing and are very unlikely to catch on.

At a meeting for a job with Alfred Holt & Co, shortly after he had left the employment of Messrs. J. H. Worthington

& Co, he is asked, "Are you a teetotaller, Captain?" and he replies that he is not and occasionally enjoys a glass. He does not say how big a glass or how often he enjoyed one, but on the evidence elsewhere he is not unfamiliar with 'good French brandy', or whiskey, which he describes as 'the universal drink in the East', as well as good quality cigars. His interviewer replies that he is pleased to hear that, because the company could not honestly welcome a man in Command who did not enjoy a tipple and thereby share a common pleasure with his crew. And as in every organization, once the crew have got against you, there is no way on earth that the situation can be remedied except by the Captain's being replaced— John Goodwin's opinion, not mine. This seems very contemporary in tone.

On the imperial front he acknowledges that men like himself have a status and authority in the East out of all proportion to their numbers. John Goodwin is sailing the South China seas at the same time as Joseph Conrad, who also recognizes in his novels and stories the disproportionate impact of these men from the West turning up at Eastern ports with purpose and organization, telegraphy, a dedication to road and port building, track laying and much else: in short, their nautical power and wealth. A brief comment he makes to an American journalist in around 1910 suggests that one shipping line alone, that of Alfred Holt & Co, his own company, had 50 huge liners traversing the globe, from Tacoma in the USA to Liverpool to Perim in the Red Sea and Yokohama in Japan, a non-stop trading of people and commodities that we, a century later, now think of as globalization. Stationed in the port of Dalny (variously described as Russian or Chinese) John Goodwin reflects on this new world and only says that it has a 'sublime incongruity'—his ship, the British ship Telemachus, in a Russian-built port, lit by American lighting, delivering English locomotives destined for the Manchurian railroad. He looks round him in wonder, left only with the thought that the chief steward on board is also likely to be playing 'Abide With Me' or 'Waltz Me Round Again, Willie' on the gramophone.

In 'A Survivor Found At Sea' we read of a young man adrift in a small boat in the Indian Ocean, 1,000 miles off-course, the First Mate already dead of hunger and thirst, pushed into the sea, the Captain also dead, but alas decomposing in front of his eyes in a little cuddy. Remarkably the young man is still alive and we find out from his subsequent account that he has been drifting for four months. We can't help being astonished by the experience of that young man, 19-year-old Josue Green, four months on the 'wide wide sea' of the Indian Ocean, eating raw fish and drinking sea water. But for the sheer chance of being spotted and rescued by the Telemachus, under the captaincy of John Henry Goodwin, these three souls would have gone into the void of the disappeared altogether, ones who vanish from the face of the earth and are never seen again. They had previously been passed by two ships which didn't take them on.

At 62, still in his ship Telemachus, John Goodwin leaves Liverpool for Jeddah where he picks up 1,000 pilgrims on their way back to the Far East after the Hajj.

He arrives in Penang (Malaysia) and notes that on the voyage eight of the pilgrims have become sick and died, which is compensated for by a live birth, although this in itself is somewhat spoiled by two factions of Malays getting into a serious fracas with knives and axes. This seems par for the course, life and death on each hand. It is not surprising that towards the end of his career, having survived forty-odd years at sea, John Goodwin is described by the American journalist as having a certain 'geniality'.

Do sailors live on in the afterlife? In John Henry Goodwin's case they do. He spends the first three months of his retirement feverishly resting up, after which he is back in the maritime business with a vengeance, this time as a 'nautical advisor' for Alfred Holt & Co. From there he throws himself into the Mercantile Marine Service Association set up in 1917 against a backdrop of union action for better pay. He gets himself elected to one committee after another, sub-committee after sub-committee, and becomes the President, all the time bringing his great experience of sailors and sailing to bear upon the land-lubbing boys of Whitehall and the shipping lines whose only hold on reality is a figure on a slide rule. By 1919 he has helped to establish uniform rates of pay for 'common seamen'—a task, as he says, easily achieved—and in addition for Masters and Captains, whose pay had always been a jealously guarded secret. In 1919, at the height of his power and influence, he is offered and accepts an MBE for civil services to government.

You can't help feeling that the old man (by this time he is 69) is really rather pleased with national recognition for a life he had chosen anyway. Nevertheless, having received the award he takes a great deal of pride in being invited to meetings in Liverpool Town Hall with the Mayor, admirals, peers and politicians, and on another occasion to attend a River Thames pageant where he finds himself—to his surprise—hobnobbing with the greatest in the land.

It is a strange afterlife, lacking romance and chaos, lacking the incongruous and the exotic, lacking the unpredictability of the sea. His youngest daughter Bessie moves to Australia to marry a former Liverpudlian there; Carrie, his first daughter, lost the man she had hoped to marry in the war, and she and her younger sister, Meg, whose husband died during the Spanish Flu epidemic, subsequently move back in with them at their house in Bootle. The house lease coming up for renewal, the old tar looks round for somewhere to buy outright and ends up in Seaforth, which he notes with regret has small rooms and takes him and his wife some getting used to. At the end of this period he gives up the voluntary work he had thrown himself into when he had had the strength. His 'Continued Memoirs of Captain J.H. Goodwin of Liverpool' from which I have taken this information is signed off in July 1928. He lived a further two years of which nothing is known.

One of the many touching sides of his character is the hope he often expresses that one day his descendants will read his story of life at sea. His son, also a John Henry, inhabited a world which so neatly dovetailed with his own, as nautical engineer, that he may not have thought it worth his while reading about it. He seems to look through to his grandsons instead, all four of them, only one of whom went to sea, and I will mention their names now to show that the old sailor's aspirations to family immortality were not an illusion. They are, in birth order, Leslie John Royce Goodwin ('Jack') [1907 – 1998], Sydney Royce Goodwin ('Sid') [1908 – 1968], William Dunstan Royce Goodwin ('Roy') [1914 – 1974] and George Stanley Goodwin ('Young George') [1927 – 1986]. These have now passed along the way of the good Captain himself.

Jack Goodwin, the eldest of the brothers, married Janet Neil from Scotland and in turn passed the manuscript to their eldest daughter, Jean Goodwin (now O'Connell) in the hope that she would manage to do something with it which he had been unable to do. She still has it, but here the story of the manuscript ends, because we now live in a wonderfully savvy internet-enabled age, full of gizmos and devices, pop-ups and downloads, machines on the blink, but where the opportunities to see a book into print are easier than ever before. The clatter of Minnie Mitchell's typewriter of 1915 is no more, and only for an older generation of us is that cheerful sound still a memory.

But the Life At Sea (1865 – 1915) by John Henry Goodwin is now a fact, and it fulfils a Victorian mariner's dream of seeing his experiences set down for all to read. We may not see the 'wide wide sea' as he did, except through his eyes, but no-one can fail to share with him his voyage through history and time.

# Acknowledgements

Many thanks are due to Dave Peden who scanned the foolscap manuscript in and worked to provide the first readable copy in an electronic format. Dave designed the cover, using a photograph of John Goodwin, and also set the entire book ready for printing. Thanks also to John Saunders (incidentally the nephew of Janet Neil mentioned above) who kindly agreed to proof-read the final copy and who made invaluable suggestions about style and presentation.

For myself I would like to say that I have kept all of John Goodwin's chapters as they were. I have deleted one or two paragraphs where the same events are recounted in other parts; I have moved one or two paragraphs around for logical reasons to support the narrative. For a similar reason I have disengaged several paragraphs of conversation and put each line of speech separately; this is more familiar to us, is clearer to read, and I am sure the Captain would not demur.

John Goodwin frequently dignifies common words like Salt and Tobacco with capital letters, which gives them an importance they no longer seem to have. I have kept them throughout. Wisely or unwisely, I have also kept now-historic words like 'Japs' and spellings like 'Hindoo' which some may find pejorative. No-one escapes the language and attitudes of his time, and none more so than John Goodwin whose occasional diatribes against the Welsh or the Irish, anyone in fact who is not English and Protestant, are sometimes hard to stomach. Here and there I have put brief explanations [in square brackets] where place-names have changed or where words entirely commonplace to him have left our vocabulary.

Finally, in line with memories of books I read in my own childhood in the 1950s, I have given at the head of each chapter a brief indication of episodes or events contained therein. These to me evoke the spirit of those childhood books, and hence of an earlier age of reading and expression, and also as I found for myself is a useful means of looking up individual parts without having to spend ages thumbing through the whole work. The rest is the book as he wrote it.

John Comer
2013

# Chapter 1

*1850 Born in Liverpool—ghosts in the house—*
*New York in the Civil War—bound apprentice to*
*Messrs. T & J Brocklebank—marriage—shipwrecked*

I, JOHN HENRY GOODWIN, eldest son of Edward J. Goodwin (who was fifth son of John and Rebecca (Hoyle) Goodwin) was born in Birkenhead on the 8th June 1850, and when I was two years of age my parents removed to Liverpool, residing in the District of Toxteth Park then practically suburban.

The difficulty in writing one's life from memory is that after you have written up a certain portion, items of interest are bound to occur to your mind, hence the following little stories of my early life.

When I was six years old I had golden hair, which our mother kept in curls, much to my disgust, and I remember my father on coming home from sea saying to my mother, "Mary, don't you think it time you made a boy of that child, and cut off those curls", but she would not hear of it. However, a day or two after my father took me out, curls and all for a walk, I came back minus curls, to my delight and my mother's disgust.

In the early part of the year 1858, the servant girl took my brother and I out for a walk, taking us to a clay-pit to show us how to catch sticklebacks. I fell in, and was nearly drowned. I can just remember being led home by a policeman like a drowned rat, in a great funk, and a procession of youngsters following. We then lived in a house in Park Road—for some months only. We had to leave it because it was haunted, no tenant would stay in it, yet the house is standing now (1906), having been turned into a shop. It was a three-storied house with a cellar kitchen. On the top floor there were three rooms, a small one which mother kept as a sort of box and store room, the front room where I and my brother slept, and in the back room the servant maid. One evening in early summer—say about 8 o'clock—servant out and just getting dusk, we youngsters in bed, and mother tucking us in for the night, she had just previously put her bunch of keys in the store-room door, and while sitting by the bedside talking to me she suddenly stopped and said, "Do you hear anything, John?"

"Yes," I said, "someone came out of the store-room and is going downstairs."

With that she jumped up and started to follow, and whatever it was went straight down to the kitchen, mother following to the top of the kitchen stairs, and then she funked, shut the landing door and opened the front door and knocked up our neighbours, who came in. They went into the kitchen and found both back door and area door bolted on the inside and no-one there. Fancy, you say. Oh no, absolute fact! We could hear the furniture being pulled about often, but never saw anything, and we had to leave the house. Mother and I often talked about the matter afterwards, and while I may say here that I am no believer in vulgar ghosts, yet I do believe there are happenings in houses that have never been explained. I have had, or my family have had, a much later experience of a haunted house, in which we lived nine years and had to leave as the manifestations became unbearable. Perhaps I may be able to get my wife or eldest daughter to write up their experience of this house. If so, it will be attached to this later on. Just now, I refrain from mentioning the road in which the house stands, but it is in Bootle.

One of my earliest recollections is mother receiving a letter from my father's sister—Ellen Vincent Goodwin—conveying the news of her brother Robert's death in America. My father being at sea in Command of a wooden ship called Helen in the Quebec trade, she being the vessel in which he first went to sea, and strange to say while still under his Command she was waterlogged and abandoned at sea in the winter of 1858, all hands being saved. In that year my sister Eleanor was born, and my sister Rebecca died of Scarlet Fever, myself and my brother Edward both taking it, and having a very close call.

In March 1861, my father being then in Command of the S.S. Zulu, carrying the English mail between Jamaica and New York, my mother, myself, and Annie—my youngest sister, then a baby in arms—sailed from Liverpool in the S.S. City of Washington, 1,400 tons register, for New York, taking up our residence there, I going to a public school for some five months. This was at the beginning of the American Civil War, and during this time I saw some stirring scenes, such as the departure of troops for the front—the great excitement after the Battle of Bull Run, in which the Northern

Army was defeated—the return of the 69th New York Irish Regiment, who covered the retreat at that Battle.

I also saw the great procession escorting the body of the so-called martyr, Colonel Ellsworth [first notable Union soldier to die in the Civil war] who was shot while pulling down the so-called rebel flag which was flying over the Hotel in Baltimore, the same having been hoisted by the keeper—Jackson—who was a Southern sympathiser, and who shot Ellsworth on his rushing up to haul down the flag. Excessive zeal cost the latter his life. His proper course should have been to order a squad of soldiers to occupy the hotel and pull down the flag.

In September 1861, my father having unfortunately lost his ship on a reef in the West Indies, the family returned to England in October of the same year, by the S.S. City of Glasgow. I then went to school until the age of 13 (the girl, who afterwards became my wife, going to the Girls' side of the same school) and being of a restless disposition, and wanting to go to sea, my parents thinking to cure me of my desire, placed me in a Cotton Broker's Office in Chapel Street, Liverpool. During the 16 months I was there, I witnessed many exciting scenes on the Exchange, when the news of battles lost and won in the Civil War in the United States came to hand. We had no submarine cable then. The old Liverpool Exchange was then standing pretty much on the same site as that now occupied by the present building, the West side of Rumford Street being all warehouses.

In the winter of 1864, I took a small part in one of the largest, if not the last, Snowball Fights that ever took place on the Liverpool Exchange. This good-humoured fight took place between merchants, brokers, and clerks on the one hand, and all and sundry citizens on the other, and the so-called riot was not subdued until the Reserve Police and Fire Brigade with hoses arrived. I think the Public Houses did well after the Fire Brigade were through with the crowd, and the West India Rum Trade benefited—Rum hot, being the drink in those days. About 100 unfortunates were arrested, and I saw one well-known Liverpool Cotton Broker (who only died in 1900) being led off by two policemen, he protesting loudly. All the above were fined and cautioned. Some people said it was disgraceful, but for my part I thought the fight jolly good fun. There were 'Peace at any price' people, and 'Little Englanders' even in those days.

In November 1865 much against the wishes of my poor Mother, but with her reluctant consent, I was bound as a sea apprentice for 4½ years to Messrs. T & J Brocklebank of Liverpool, they undertaking to have me taught the duties of a seaman, and I undertaking to serve my Masters day and night both afloat and ashore.

On the 16th November 1865 I sailed out of the old George's Basin (now filled up) in the good ship Comorin, 804 tons register, bound for Calcutta, under the Command of Captain Frank Wise, as fine a seaman, as warm a friend, and as crotchety a gentleman as ever sailed the sea. One of his pet aversions was Tobacco in any form. Nothing used to please him more than to catch one of us boys with a chew of Tobacco in our mouth. He would stand us on the quarter deck—the sacred place on board a ship—and say, "Now you young rascal, spit if you dare," and when we did have to spit, our breakfast or dinner went over the lee rail with the quid of Tobacco. Then the old gentleman would grin and say, "There, that will teach you to chew dirty filthy Tobacco." Dear old man, I owe him, or his memory, a deep debt of gratitude. He taught me my business, and it was to his kindly interest and help in teaching me navigation that I owe my present position.

My first experience at sea as a worker was a rough one. Some two hours after leaving Liverpool, a man fell overboard, but was fortunately rescued, and I was very much shocked by the Captain saying to the man as he was pulled aboard half drowned, "You d----- fool, what did you fall overboard for?" Well, we went on, and for three weeks were buffeted by one of the most tempestuous spells of weather ever experienced round the Coast of England. At the end of the three weeks, we were just 300 miles from Liverpool. During one of the heaviest blows we had, with the Barometer down to 28.30, a man fell off the fore topsail yard arm, while close reefing the topsail. He fell clear of the ship and a big sea carried him aft into the mizzen chains, where he hung on shouting for help. We got him aboard and the next day he was on duty, a providential escape, and one which made a great impression on me, though it did not make me swallow the anchor (a nautical term for giving up the sea).

On the 12th August 1866, I returned to Liverpool, a sunburnt, tar-ry sailor, thinking myself no end of a swell, and received a warm welcome from my dear mother, who alas was never to welcome her sailor boy home again, for she died on the 12th December of the same year, while I was on my second voyage to Calcutta.

In 1868 my father was married again—to a Miss Jane Rose. I fully agreed with him that it was the right thing to do, if only for the sake of my two young sisters, my brother Edward having by this time gone to sea in the same line as myself. I never got on with my stepmother, and in 1870, after my father's death, I left the old roof-tree and struck out for myself, at the same time passing my examination for second mate, and then paying a visit to my Uncle John in Dublin, I having visited him in 1862 at Christmas time, spending the Christmas Day with his cousins Brown, and my Uncle John, Aunt Ellen, cousins John and Emma Goodwin.

After passing my examination, I was appointed fourth officer of my old ship the Comorin, but under another Captain. After making one voyage in her to Calcutta, I joined a fine iron ship called the Chinsura as fourth officer, being promoted to third officer through the death of the Captain, who died in my arms 19 days after leaving Liverpool. On our return to Liverpool, my old Captain, F. Wise, joined us, I retaining my position as third mate for 2½ voyages, then being lent to the ship Star Of Erin as second mate for the voyage home to London. On arriving there my old employers—Messrs. Brocklebank—appointed me second officer of their ship Arracan, bound to Hong Kong. On joining her I found an old friend and shipmate was Chief Officer of her. His name was Robert Nelson. He was a warm and close friend, and as gallant and capable a seaman as ever walked a deck. Years after, he was in Command of one of the same Company's steamers in which I now have the honour to serve (Messrs. Alfred Holt). He died at home about August 1896, leaving a wife and four children, who are to this day close friends of my family. I made one voyage to China in the Arracan, arriving home in January 1874. Before sailing on the last mentioned voyage, my sweetheart (and now dear wife) and self had made up our minds to get married on my return, I to pass my examination as Chief Mate before marriage.

Now time is short with a deep-water sailor, so I arranged to pass on the 8th of February, and get married on the 11th—being quite confident of success—but to my dismay I failed in the last given problem in navigation, and was put back for four days. I did not fail in getting married on the 11th February 1874, thinking it a pity to disappoint the Parson and Registrar, who were both ready. We were married in Shaw Street Presbyterian Church, Liverpool, by the Rev. Doctor Graham, my wife's maiden name being Emily Caroline McCulloch Williamson, her father's family belonging to Kirkcudbright, and her mother's family to Borgue, Wigtownshire. The McCulloch blood is said to be the oldest in Scotland, so my wife being a McCulloch on her mother's side must have transmitted a few drops to her children, so what with the old Saxon Goodwin blood—a dash of Welsh through the Hoyles, not forgetting the Irish connection, I think my children may be called pure British, and I wish from my heart that the whole of Great Britain would sink the race distinction, and become one in heart under the name of British.

However, on the day following my marriage, I went up and passed my examination with flying colours, and in a few days started off to London to join my ship, my wife accompanying me, and after being in London a week my wife received a telegram asking her to come home at once, as her sister Maggie, who had just been confined of twins was given up by the Doctors. I sent her off by the first available train, but she arrived too late to see her sister alive. My wife took charge of the twins, the elder child being cared for by her grandmother.

I got down to Liverpool for one night before sailing to bid my wife Good-bye, and on the 4th March 1874, sailed in the Arracan for Hong Kong, and on the night of the 8th March was run into and sunk by a steamer off the Bill of Portland, the crew barely escaping with their lives. It was my watch on deck, though the Captain was then in charge. I was thus dressed, but my brother officer—R. Nelson—was only in his underclothes. Our only available boat being crowded by the crew, there was no room in her for the Captain, mate, and myself. I said to Nelson, "This is going to be a near squeak, old chap," and he said, "Alright sonny, we will stick together, sink or swim," but to our delight we heard someone hailing in the dark, and soon saw a boat pushing towards us, into which we got, our vessel sinking soon after we got clear of her. We were taken on board of the Steamer and conveyed to Southampton, and there packed off to London by the Shipwrecked Mariners' Society, destitute, hungry, no tobacco, and clothed like pirates. We arrived in London (Waterloo Station) at midnight in a snowstorm, through which we had to tramp some four miles before reaching the Sailors' Home, Wells Street. There they took us in and fed us. After a day or two's detention, I got down to Liverpool, remaining home about two months (during which time the twins mentioned above, died) when I was called to London to give evidence at the Admiralty Courts in the case of Arracan v S.S. Syria—the Arracan winning the case.

# Chapter 2

*1865 A sailor's life—food on board—graveyards in
Calcutta—the Comorin and the Arracan*

Before I go on with my memoirs, it might be interesting
to those of my descendants who may read this if I give
them some idea of what a sailor boy's life was like when
I went to sea. Well, we lived hard, dressed hard, and
worked hard, and I am afraid we sometimes swore
hard, but the latter must not be taken as depravity, but
as a coarse rough way of speaking. When the Captain
would sing out to the helmsman, "Luff, Sir, luff, and be
damned to you," he did not mean to damn him either
soul or body, but to emphasize his order, and so reader,
you must deal charitably with the memory of the dead
and gone sailors.

The Beef (salt) supplied us in those days was of the
poorest description, being shins and shoulders packed
in Hamburg, destitute of fat, but not free from the
suspicion of being old Horse, which was what the sailors
called it. The Pork was Newfoundland fish fed, and all
fat, mostly reasty and rancid. We got 1½ lbs of Beef four
times a week and 1¼ lbs Pork three times a week, but
when I say half the Beef was bone, and half the Pork
rancid fat, there was not much left to feed a hungry boy
on. In addition to the above, we got 1 lb of Biscuits a
day, ¹/₃ rd of a pint of Peas three times a week, and ½ lb
of Flour four times, ⅛ th of an ounce of Tea and ¼ oz of
Coffee daily, and 1 lb of Sugar per week.

11

Oh the Sugar! Many a time I have had to put a piece of gauze over my tin cup, place the sugar on it, pouring the Tea or Coffee over it, and so strain out the mud and cockroach legs and sundry other insects that had their dwelling place there.

We got Bully Soup on Sunday with possibly a small piece of Meat in it, which the boatswain and carpenter—who messed with us—used to collar, until we struck, and told them we would lick them and chop them up for 'Dogs Body' (a favourite sailor's dish made of pounded bread, pork fat, and molasses) if they did not share. I guess they shared all right—12 big lads wanted some handling. We never saw a Potato or Butter or vegetable of any sort, nor had we ever a savoury dish made for us. I used to go bare-footed and bare-headed on board the ship, and would never go aloft in bad weather with seaboots on. If too cold for bare feet, I put on a pair of woollen socks with canvas soles, and when the cry of "Hands shorten sail" ran along from man to man, your humble servant was aloft like a monkey, out on the weather yard arm, light out the sail to windward, and then haul out to leeward my hearties, taut band and tie away.

It was always blowing when we did this, often raining, thundering and hailing, but it stirs my blood now when I think of it and makes me wish for one more taste of the old days when I stood as a young man at the top end of the topsail halyards singing, "Oh, up aloft this yard must go," the sailors singing the refrain, "Oh, Whisky for my Johnnie." I was considered a crack chanty-man in those days—alas, their day is over. My children have heard me singing some of them for their amusement.

In saying we never got Potatoes, I mean when at sea. We always got them and vegetables in lieu of Flour and Peas when in port. The thing we suffered most from was the short allowance of water, three quarts per day per man for all purposes, fancy that in the tropics! The cook took most of the water for cooking and our Tea and Coffee. Many a day I have gone half the day with my tongue half baked, and wishing 4 p.m. would come, the water being served out at that time every day, and when it was served out we dare not drink much, otherwise there would be none for the next day. On Saturday two buckets of water were served out to our mess (there were 12 of us) for washing in. This was four gallons of water to wash 12 big lads. Well, we divided it in two, and custom gave the eldest lads first turn. What it was like when it came to the sixth boy's turn, I will leave you to judge. Of course we only washed our faces, necks, and arms, we had plenty of salt water bathing for our bodies, no stint of salt-water at sea. Like the 'free lunch counter', it is 'cut and come again'. We mended and washed our own clothes, the latter with salt water except when it rained, and then we had a glorious time. We filled ourselves up inside and soaked it in from the outside. We filled all the casks we could get, but rainwater cannot be kept long in casks, it soon gets bad and tastes like rotten egg smell.

Among the many unpleasant things a sailor used to be called upon to tackle was a leaky ship. I had the misfortune to have had my share of it, down off the Cape of Good Hope or the Horn. Fighting day and night with adverse winds, standing at the pumps with the water washing up to your waist was no uncommon thing in my young days. "Pump or sink" was the cry and pump we did. Many a poor fellow suffered badly from salt water boils and Rheumatism, but thank God I was blessed with a strong constitution, and was thus able to face the music at all times.

I will just give a little story which my Father told me of one of his experiences of a sailor's life. He was second mate of a small brig, and somewhere in the South Atlantic becalmed, everything in the ship eatable used up but the bread or biscuit, and that none too good, and water scarce. He was lying in his bunk asleep and began to dream that someone was preparing him a lovely dinner—roast duck he thought. The dream was so realistic that he awoke, and Lo! the smell was a reality. Jumping out of his bunk he ran into the cabin and there at the stove was the steward with a saucepan.

"My Goodness, steward," he said, "what have you there?"

The steward answered, "If I hand you some will you eat it?"

"Eat," said my dad, "I would eat you if you smelt like that," and eat it he did, asking no questions for conscience sake. When he told me the story I said, "Well Dad, what was it?" He answered, "Rats my boy, and jolly good they were."

And now a few words about Calcutta, as it was when I first went there. The River Banks were just as God made them, except where man had built what were called 'landing Ghauts'. There were flights of steps leading up from the water, being almost 100 feet long and wide, and a favourite bathing place for the Hindoos. The River was often the colour of pea soup, but we had to drink the water all the same, as there was no other to be had for ships, the consequence being that Dysentery and Cholera were only too common amongst us. Many a fine fellow I have seen alive to-day, and in his grave before sunset the next day, only a 'common sailor', God help him.

It was the custom in India for the Hindoos either to burn their dead or to carry their sick and dying down to the River Ganges, and put them on the bank below high water mark, the rising tide washing them away—this was a sure way of going to Heaven. The Government were trying to stop it, but India is a large place, and means of communication were indifferent. I have seen daily six or seven dead men and women floating down the River with the Vultures and Kites feasting on them. The corpses would often foul our anchor chains, and we had to go and clear them away.

Many a ghastly sight I have seen, but none so utterly disgusting and ghastly as one I saw in the year 1867. I was over on the opposite side of the River to Calcutta one Sunday afternoon on a voyage of discovery on my own account, and having lost my way I stumbled on a low-walled enclosure wondering what it was. I looked round and found an entrance, into which I entered and found myself in a large compound full of heaped up dead men's skulls and bones. To say I was scared would be putting it very mildly, but seeing the compound led to the River, I screwed up my courage and walked on between the heaps of skulls, and noticing smoke rising ahead of me, I said to myself, "There are live men there anyhow," so keeping on I soon discovered three men sitting round what appeared to be an ordinary fire, but on drawing near I saw they had a dead man, half on and half off the fire, burning him piece by piece. I stood fascinated for a while, then I girded up my loins and fled the scene, only on reaching the River side to stumble on another corpse lying on the River Bank, with an Adjutant (a large carrion bird) making a meal of it. I had wandered into a poor Hindoo Burning Ground, and the Ghouls I saw sitting round the fire were what is called in India 'Doom Wallahs'. They were practically in the same position as our Undertakers, except that in India the job is hereditary, and when anyone died they gave these men a sum of money to burn them, the police also giving them so much for burning all bodies stranded on the banks of the River, and as the place I stumbled on was in a lonely place, the gentlemen economised on the fuel. I often wonder these chaps did not knock me on the head for a spy, but the stern and just lesson taught the natives after the Mutiny, was not forgotten at that time, and a white man was feared and respected.

By 1871 jetties and wharves had been built in Calcutta, and the scandals in the burning grounds had been removed, and properly appointed ovens for burning the dead had been constructed, a good water supply was being brought to the shipping and town, and by 1884 Calcutta was a Paradise compared to what it was in 1865, though Cholera was still common in the summer. In 1884 Captain John Thomas (who was eldest apprentice on the Comorin when I went to sea) went on board his ship at 8 p.m. one evening apparently quite well, and we buried him next afternoon—Cholera was the cause. But enough of horrors.

I will now say a few words about the ship Comorin. She was built in 1858 of Elm and Pitch pine, was ship rigged, three single topsail yards, and stunsails, both at main and fore. She was a fast sailer and a very weatherly ship, but leaked like a basket, and was infested with Rats. I have been lying awake in my berth and seen the deck black with rats, and I have seen them empty what is called an open Duck Lamp, by dipping their tails in, and sucking the oil off them. One night while I was sleeping, they ate the hard skin off my feet until the blood was just coming, and my toe-nails were eaten down to the quick, but I did not know that until I went on deck into the salt water. One night I had a rat under the blankets with me, and yet another time I awoke and found one sitting on my forehead performing his toilet like a cat. Which was the most surprised—the rat when he found himself landed with a thump on the deck, or me when I found him on my forehead—I don't know, but I think the rat, judging by the noise he made.

With reference to the Arracan and Comorin I may just say a few words regarding their history and which illustrates how like human beings they are, born to fortune or misfortune. The Arracan was a teak built ship, her birthplace Whitehaven, her builders and owners Messrs. T & J Brocklebank. She was what may be called an unfortunate ship. In the year 1867 there was a terrible cyclone in the Bay of Bengal. The Arracan was then lying in Sangor Roads at the mouth of the River Hooghly, outward bound from Calcutta, when the cyclone commenced. She dragged both of her anchors, drove right over a bank with little water on it, lost her three masts and brought up to her anchors in deep water as the wind abated. About six vessels were totally dismasted at Sangor that night, all of them being driven ashore, during the same hurricane. The ship Comorin in which I was then serving was, when the hurricane began, about 200 miles South of the Arracan's position, standing North with the wind about E.N.E. as near as I can remember, fresh breeze, squally looking, but apparently fine.

At 6 p.m. Captain Wise came on deck and gave the order, "All hands shorten sail," and to our amazement put her under two close reefed topsails, and kept her off S.W. with the wind a little on the starboard quarter. At midnight it was blowing a howling cyclone, the wind hauling more Northerly, and by noon next day we were standing North, wind South to S.E. with all sail set, thus showing how a knowledge of the Law of Storms can save a ship from damage. At midnight on the night of the cyclone, a London East Indiaman called the Nile with troops on board was just 30 miles from us trying to heave to, and was totally dismasted, and nearly foundered. Just after midnight or thereabouts, a steamer—a rare sight in those seas—nearly collided with us, and passed away quickly in the driving rain. She was standing to the Northward—a fatal course under the circumstances.

When we got to Calcutta, great anxiety was being displayed over the non-appearance of the S.S. Thunderer from China with some £100,000 worth of specie [currency in the form of coin] on board, she being the opium steamer. She never turned up, and there is little doubt it was her we saw. Several expeditions went into the Sunderbunds (the network of Rivers and dense Jungle which form the mouths of the River Ganges— south coast of Bengal) to look for her, but it is my opinion she foundered in deep water that night. The Arracan was again totally dismasted off Madeira about the year 1870/1871, my brother Edward then being an apprentice on her. The Comorin faded away from my ken about 1880, but I never heard of her being lost. I rather think she was broken up in the shipbreaker's yard, so "Good-bye Comorin."

I may add to the above story of the cyclone, that some 100,000 people were drowned that night on the low-lying shores of Orissa and Bengal. We sailed through a great deal of wreckage, trees, houses, cattle and human corpses, and when we got to the entrance of the River found all Light-ships, buoys, and pilot vessels gone. None of them were totally lost, but driven away and dismasted. The Pilot brigs were eventually towed into Madras. As soon as the fact of the pilots &c. being missing was known, the S.S. Courthey—probably the finest tug afloat in those days—was sent down with pilots, to take up the Eastern Channel Lightship Station. Our arrival and hers was simultaneous.

# Chapter 3

*1874 Appointed Second Officer—Master Mariner—*
*his wife described—first son born—Master of the Morna*

And now to return to my history, which left off at the Arracan's trial in 1874, after which I was appointed second officer of the ship Baroda—Captain William Ray, with Mr J. Marley, Chief Officer. We sailed in May and made a quick voyage to Calcutta, and back to Liverpool, arriving there on the 29th December, having been detained in the Crosby Channel four days by fog. It was freezing hard all the time, and I was never so cold in my life before, though I have been since.

On the 27th January 1875, my eldest daughter Emily Caroline Williamson Goodwin [Carrie'], named after her Mother, was born. She was a fine child, and by God's goodness has grown into a fine woman, tall— being 5 ft. 9 inches, blonde hair, good-looking and a regular Goodwin in physique and character, has a loving generous disposition, and inclined to be self-opinionated. She has a good constitution, is a good manager, and a clever woman when she likes, but withal a good daughter, she can be as stubborn as a mule when the fit takes her—just like her father. My daughter was born in 19 Leeds Street, Liverpool. The house has since been pulled down to make room for Railway improvements.

In February 1875 I again sailed as second officer of the Baroda, same Captain, and Chief Officer, arriving back home about October of the same year, when Mr Morley was appointed Master of the ship Mahanada, 1,001 tons register, built of teak in 1864 at Whitehaven, a noble vessel, and I felt proud on later being appointed Chief Officer of her, sailing for Calcutta in the beginning of December. We experienced some heavy weather off the Cape of Good Hope, and in the Indian Ocean encountered two hurricanes in a week, ship running before the wind, or thereabouts crossing the path of the centre, and gaining safety on the receding edge of the storm. In both cases, our sails were blown away, and I never saw anything to equal the conflict of the elements. It was raining in sheets and the sky and sea seemed to be one. For two days we could not cook anything, and things generally were dark and miserable, but by God's mercy we pulled through all right. There are a few places in the world where the war of Elements are awe-inspiring and fearful. I have seen some terrible displays of lightning and heard thunder down South of Madagascar that fairly shook the ship, and the electric storms keep on for 48 hours without cessation. There are bad electric disturbances, in the Bay of Bengal, and the Straits of Malacca, but nothing like those of Madagascar.

I arrived back in England in September 1876 and found that my wife had removed to Kirkdale, so as to be near her sister—Mrs Parry—whose husband, W. Parry, was Dock Master of the Huskisson Dock, Liverpool. In 1876 I was appointed Chief Officer of the ship Baroda,

1,436 tons register, under the Command of Captain W. Ellery, and again sailed for Calcutta, and while away on this voyage my second child was born on Sunday June 10th 1877. She was christened Margaret Jane Williamson Goodwin [known as 'Meg'] her first two names being those of my wife's two deceased sisters, and still living Aunts. Meg was a very nervous child from the first, and the most delicate of the family. She is of a very lively disposition and has borne all her troubles and sicknesses bravely and cheerfully. She is a clever housewife, and takes more after her mother than any of the others.

I returned home from this voyage in July and on the 15th August 1877, I passed my examination for Master Mariner, so the year 1877 was a somewhat eventful year for me, and I may add for my dear wife also. We married young, and I am afraid without much thought of the serious responsibilities of the married state, but we loved each other, and both of us had a fair quantity of ballast. We had a hard time in many ways, more especially my wife, for our means were limited, but we never bought anything we could do without, and never got into debt, and my wife was brave, resourceful, and clever. God was good to us, and blessed us with health and a gradually increasing success and prosperity.

Perhaps it may be well if I describe my wife, so that those of our descendants who read this may know what their ancestors were like. She is 5 ft. in height, small-boned, and plump—even as a girl—had light hair then, turning to brown. When about 40/50 years of age, blue-grey eyes, changeable in shade, is of a sweet and loving disposition, loyal to her husband, his companion and adviser, and withal a woman who learned to love, honour, and obey. She is dignified and knows when to assert herself, and brave in spirit—an elder sister to her daughters, and loved by all who know her. Now you will say, "What are her faults?" Well, I can only say, "I don't know," for I have never been able to find any, and I know our children will endorse every word I have said.

About the end of September 1877, I again sailed as Chief of the Baroda, making rather a long voyage. On account of trade being bad, we lay some four months in Calcutta, but finally reached Liverpool 18th August 1878, when I was transferred to the iron ship Majestic, 1884 tons register, a splendid vessel, and one of the largest sailing vessels afloat. She belonged to Messrs. T & J Brocklebank, and was commanded by Captain W. Ellery, a good Shipmaster from many points of view, but a very uncomfortable man to sail with. Nevertheless for my family's sake I stayed on with him, looking forward to my promotion, and making several voyages with him in the Majestic, finally arriving in London in February 1881. I could not have made another voyage with Captain Ellery, and had made up my mind to resign, Messrs. Brocklebank not having any vacancy for Master then. While I was still in a state of uncertainty as to my future movements, my old friend Captain W. Ray—then Messrs. Brocklebank's Overlooker—introduced me to Messrs. Joseph Hall Worthington & Co, who were in want of a Master for their ship Morna, and to my joy and delight, they appointed me to her at once.

Before entering on an account of my career as Master,

I must go back to Tuesday, the 17th of June 1879, on which my dear wife presented me with a son, who in due time was christened in St. Aidan's Church, Kirkdale, and named John Henry Williamson Goodwin. My brother Edward was his Godfather. He was a strong lusty child, but when about 14 months old, he got inflammation of the Bowels, which kept him back considerably. He however picked up, and became strong and lusty.

About this time my brother Edward joined Messrs. Alfred Holt's China steamers as third officer, and in the following year was married to Mary Jane Brown, of Liverpool.

I was appointed Master of the ship Morna in March 1881. She was a fine iron ship, built in 1878 by Messrs. Laird of Birkenhead, 1,440 tons register, and a moderately fast sailer, but too heavily sparred. Nevertheless I was very successful in her, and commanded her until October 1890—my reasons for leaving her will be given later on in these Memoirs.

When I got Command the Morna was lying in Bristol, having gone there with a cargo of Wheat from San Francisco. After discharge I took her to Penarth and Cardiff, to load coal for Calcutta. My wife and son accompanied me to both these ports, staying with me until I sailed. My wife who bad been suffering from fever and ague derived much good from the change.

We sailed on the 30th April 1881 for Calcutta, making the passage in 90 days, and the round voyage back to Liverpool in 7 months 10 days. It was the quickest and best paying voyage the Morna had ever made, and my reputation as a Shipmaster was at once established, and by God's goodness has since been maintained.

It may be interesting to my readers to hear the rates of freight then ruling from Calcutta, and which we secured in the Morna. Saltpetre and Sugar were 50/-, Castor Oil £4. 5. 0., Jute (light) £3.15. 0., Tea £3.15. 0., and other light freight averaging about the some rate. In 1906 Jute was being brought from Calcutta to Dundee for 21/- per ton of 50 feet, a great reduction, in fact I think too great, for the labourer is worthy of his hire.

While away on this voyage my wife removed to Grove Street, Bootle, her Mother and Minnie Mitchell (her sister Maggie's child) living with her. It is Minnie who has typed my Memoirs for me, and corrected any mistakes I have made in spelling and grammar, mistakes that old sailors are too prone to make, but what can be expected from a man who knew more about a marling-spike than a pen when a lad.

And now eight bells has gone, and the watch called, I think I will conclude this portion of my Memoirs, trusting later on to continue them.

# Chapter 4

Speaking of my arrival home from off my first voyage, as Master, I can never forget the welcome I received from my wife and children. They did not expect me for about three weeks, so my readers can imagine what a joyful surprise my arrival was to them. It was a dark foggy evening when I got to the door of my new home, which I had not yet seen. Knocking at the door, it was opened by Minnie Mitchell, then about ten years old. I said, "Does Mrs Goodwin live here?"

Minnie looked at me for a while, and then burst out with, "Auntie, Auntie, Uncle, Uncle." Almost simultaneously with her cry, I heard the frou-frou of a woman's skirts whisking down stairs, doors flung open, a joyful yell from three lusty young throats, and my wife was in my arms, the children hanging on to me, and my wife's dear mother walking round us like a cooper round a cask. It was a glorious welcome, and would pay any man for the separation of long months at sea. How proud my wife and her mother were. They had been anxious and worried about me, bad weather having prevailed off the Coasts, and one of my owner's ships from Calcutta had gone missing. It was my first voyage as Captain, with all the responsibilities and cares of that position, but in a moment their cares had been taken from them and all was joy and peace.

The missing vessel referred to was called the Eblana which sailed from Calcutta about six weeks before I did, and I regret to say was never heard of again. This disappearing of ships at sea was more common than most people suppose. In February 1880, the ship Bay of Biscay—in which my wife's nephew, James Parry was serving his apprenticeship—disappeared with all hands. We know there was very bad weather in the Atlantic, and she must have foundered during the heavy gales which prevailed.

On my arrival home from this, my second voyage in the Morna, I found that my brother Edward had met with an accident, a bar of iron slipped from a sling while discharging from the steamer he was second officer of, she then lying in the Port of Penang. The bar of iron pierced his right lung, but after six weeks in Penang Hospital he got home safely. Unfortunately an abscess formed, and he had to go into the Royal Southern Hospital to be operated on, remaining there some nine months before he was fit to go out. During his stay in Hospital, be got congestion of the Kidneys, and Malaria Fever, the latter of course being an old trouble brought on again by weakness. He was dangerously ill when I sailed on my third voyage, and there was faint hope of his recovery, so you may be sure, reader, that I left home with a sad and sorrowful heart, for I loved my brother well, though we had seen but little of each other since boyhood. He was a bright cheerful fellow, and a real good Christian man. On coming out of the Hospital, he was appointed by Messrs. Alfred Holt & Co, as Assistant Overlooker in Birkenhead for their steamers, a position he filled for ten years, and served a further ten years as Overlooker in Glasgow, where he died.

After being home a month and loading a cargo of Salt, I sailed for Calcutta on the 27th January 1882, arriving there on the 12th May. We left again for Liverpool on July 1st, in tow of a tug called the Enterprise which was engaged to tow us down the River Hooghly, but we encountered strong tidal eddies off Fulta Point, and my ship and the tug came into collision, doing considerable damage to both, necessitating our returning to Calcutta for repairs, sailing again on the 16th July. We had a very bad passage down the Bay of Bengal, the heaviest monsoon I have ever seen prevailing. However we arrived at Liverpool 25th October 1882, after a passage of 99 days. During my stay in Liverpool, I met the builder of my ship, Mr William Laird, who complimented me upon the good passages I had made in the Morna.

We loaded a cargo of coal at Birkenhead, and sailed 28th November 1882 for Rangoon, arriving there March 9th 1883—passage 101 days. We were chartered to load Rice for Liverpool, but the charterers falling, we went to Calcutta and loaded a cargo of Jute for Dundee, at a much better rate of freight, but the shifting of ports was expensive. I had several new experiences in Rangoon, but though some of them were amusing, I fear I cannot relate them, as my memories are hanging fire, and I am making no more progress than a cloud in a calm, so I must check in my weather braces, ease off my tacks, and let her run free for a while.

After duly loading our cargo of Jute, we sailed for home, the anchor coming up to the cathead to the song of the sailors, viz.

*We are homeward bound, that is the sound,*
*Good-bye fare-you-well, good-bye fare-you-well,*
*We're homeward bound for Liverpool Town,*
*Hurrah my boys, we're homeward bound.*

On this passage we experienced very bad weather off the Cape of Good Hope. Twice the ship was hove down by the gale almost on her beam ends, and both times I had to run her back before the wind until it moderated, and altogether we got such a dressing down that I thought we had usurped the functions of the Flying Dutchman, indeed some of the more superstitious of the crew swore they saw his vessel. However, we arrived at Dundee in October, my wife and son—the latter then about five years of age—joining me there. We were ordered round to Cardiff, and my wife being a bad sailor, I determined to send her by train. Our sailing day was the 10th November, and on awakening from sleep in the morning, I found it was blowing from the S.W. and increasing to a gale. On going down to the Docks, I met the Captain of a ship called the Cathcart, also ready to sail for Cardiff. After comparing notes and opinions about the weather, we decided not to go that tide. I ordered my crew down for the night's tide, but the other Captain did not, holding that the weather would be worse.

I said, "Well if it is, we can go home again."

At 3 o'clock in the afternoon the wind shifted to N.N.W. and at 9 p.m. I sailed, making the passage round to Cardiff in four days, but unfortunately, I had to lie in the Roads for ten days before Docking, the Docks being full, and nothing coming out, owing to the continuous heavy gales. The Cathcart sailed the morning after I did, and took six weeks to get to Cardiff, thus showing the importance of being ready to seize the first change of wind when in a sailing ship.

I will now relate a case in point while in the ship Majestic. We left Liverpool in tow of the S.S. Wrestler, a paddle tug. A smaller ship than mine left at the same time for Calcutta in tow of a twin-screw tug called the Stormcock, then quite new. It blew a hard gale from the S.W. and the Wrestler hung on to us all night off Holyhead, the Stormcock took her tow into the Harbour, being unable to hold her on. At daylight the wind shifted to N.W. and we got across to the Irish land, and so down to Tuskar, making one of the quickest voyages on record to Calcutta, viz. 71 days. Five weeks after, the other ship arrived, we passing her off the Pilot Station entrance to the River Hooghly, we homeward bound, she still outward bound. She had been wind-bound in Holyhead for a week, and so missed the favourable winds. At that time there was great difference of opinion as to whether paddle or twin-screw was the best for tow-boats. I myself have always considered a paddle-boat the best for deep-sea towing, but of course there are many other reasons why the twin-screws have superseded the paddle.

My wife, son, two daughters, and Minnie Mitchell, joined me in Cardiff, and there as a family we spent our first Christmas Day together—indeed I had never spent one with my wife. Think of that 'Ye Land-lubbers' who live at home at ease. The Christmas mentioned was the 25th December 1883—a red letter day to me.

I sailed for Calcutta 10th January 1884, making a passage of 119 days, and left again for New York June 14th 1884, arriving there September 29th 1884, just 23 years since I had been there before. I at once telegraphed for my wife, and she came over in the S.S. Arizona, the then 'Atlantic Flier'. The wife brought over our son John with her. He was a fine little fellow, but it took all hands and the Cook to keep him from killing or drowning himself.

# Chapter 5

*1884 New York—Bombay—San Francisco—*
*second daughter born—a seal discovered—finding a crew*
*in San Francisco—crimping*

During my stay in New York I had the pleasure of meeting my Aunt, Elizabeth Goodwin, and my uncle Henry Goodwin, who came from Charleston, West Virginia, to see us. He was a most lovable man, and a gentleman from head to foot. My wife quite fell in love with him, but alas it was the first and last time we were to see either of them, for both Uncle Henry and Aunt Bessie were dead when we visited New York four years later. I also had letters from my Aunt Julia Bryson (my father's sister), and her eldest son, William Bryson, came from Chicago to visit us. He is a fine fellow and as the Americans say, 'One of Nature's Gentlemen'. My wife was delighted with him, but as we meet him later on, I will give him a stand easy.

After a very pleasant time in New York, I had again to part from my dear wife, she going home in the White Star steamer Republic sailing on the 20th November 1884, and on the 21st November I sailed for Bombay with a cargo of Case Oil, making a passage of five months and five days, arriving April 27th 1885. This passage was so long that we came on the overdue list, so it can be quite understood the state my poor wife was in. The cause of our long passage was calms and light winds. I found

Bombay a very fine City—indeed the finest Eastern City I had ever seen. It was not then the Plague-stricken City it has since become. We loaded a cargo of Linseed for Amsterdam, arriving there in October 1885, and as the cross-Channel steamers then came to Rotterdam, I went there to meet my wife. After a month in Amsterdam, my wife returned home and I sailed for Cardiff to load Coal and Coke for San Francisco. My wife and children joined me at Cardiff, and they to this day look back with pleasure on their stay there. I dare say some will wonder why I never took my wife round in the ship. Well, she is a poor sailor and is so bad that I get scared about her, and as she is the dearest thing on earth to me, I don't want to help her out of it.

I sailed for San Francisco on the 10th December 1885, arriving April 24th 1886, passage 135 days. On looking for homeward employment, we found that shippers had determined to force down rates. I was offered 38/- per ton, which I promptly cabled to my owners. They refused this offer, and in conjunction with other shipowners decided to lay their ship up, so after discharge was completed, I ballasted my ship and took her over to a little place called Saucelito, to lay up. The Village of Saucelito lies on the North side of San Francisco Bay, and at the time I am writing of, was a better class summer resort for San Francisco people. I became acquainted with quite a number of people, both American and English, and I must say they gave me a good time, picnics, drives, shooting parties, and social entertainments lasted the whole of the seven months we were there.

It was the custom for sailors to desert their ships at San Francisco, and mine were no exception to the rule, so we had only the apprentices (six) and the officers on board, and of course the cook and steward, for eating and drinking has to go on. The people were very kind to all on board, and I personally can say I never had a better time in my life. There were three other vessels lying in Saucelito Bay at the same time; the Garfield— Captain Thompson, who is now in Command of a White Star steamer; the Copley—Captain Sextant, and an American ship called the Standard. Her Captain (whose name was Percy), his wife and family became great friends of mine, but alas, they have all gone to their long home.

On Friday, August 27th 1886, my wife presented me with another daughter, who was in due time christened Mary Elizabeth, after my mother, and both our aunts.

On the 1st December, I received orders to go to Portland, Oregon, and sailed from San Francisco on the 4th December, arriving Portland December 19th, having been driven off to sea by bad weather for nine days after taking on board the Portland pilot. I left Portland January 8th with a load of Wheat for Queenstown, there receiving orders to proceed to Antwerp. Just a few words on our passage, before saying more of Antwerp. We were 68 days to Cape Horn, which was passed in fine Northerly weather, then the clerk of the weather having surprised us with a fine week, thought it time for a change, and we got it with a vengeance in the shape of S.W. and N.W. gales, then we got into the ice, and from 52° S. and 47° W. to Latitude 46° S. and Longitude 42° W., we passed through a continuous string of icebergs and broken ice, some 300 feet high, and others only ten feet. It was an anxious time for me, but I am thankful to say we pulled through alright.

We arrived at Antwerp June 15th 1887, the wife and all the children joining me there, and I saw my new daughter for the first time, a fine child, of whom I will speak later on. 1887 was Queen Victoria's Jubilee year, and a hot dry year it was. My daughters say now they had the finest time at Antwerp they ever had when young, and I don't doubt it for one moment, judging from the trouble they gave us.

Unfortunately our pleasure was marred by the death of my wife's dear mother. The wife and I went to Liverpool at once, leaving the children in charge of the Chief Officer's wife, except the baby, who we took with us, and she cried all the way to Liverpool. We buried my wife's mother—Mrs Williamson—in the necropolis, and then went back to Antwerp, taking Minnie Mitchell with us. At Antwerp we part loaded for San Francisco, and then crossed over to London River and loaded up with Cement at a place called Swanscombe. We had quite a nice time there, the Hop Gardens being just ready for picking, the country looked lovely, but all good things come to an end, and about the last week in August I sailed, having first sent my wife and family to Liverpool. We had a rough time off Cape Horn, and for three weeks we were doing little else but beating against adverse gales.

Speaking of fish stories, I will relate one which will probably make some people think I am drawing the long bow, but the incident is a true one. During one of the short intervals between the gales mentioned, we were lying becalmed off the South-east end of Staten Island, probably ten miles off shore. The sun had just set, but it was quite light, when we heard on our starboard beam a noise like the crying of a child. Naturally all hands had their attention drawn to the quarter from whence the sound came. Presently we observed a black head in the water coming towards us, keeping right on until it reached the ship's side, and then I saw it was a Seal, the poor brute seemed in distress, and tried to get on board the ship. The crew were in a great state of excitement and wanted to harpoon it, but I soon stopped that, and had a stage lowered close to the water, and the poor beast crying and whining all the time crawled on to the stage and lay quiet for about two hours, when it came on to blow, and the rolling of the ship soon threw it off, and we saw it no more. I think it must have been a young Seal, which had lost the herd to which it belonged.

However that may be, an incident like the foregoing might easily in a more superstitious age have given rise to the mermaid yarns. I have always had strong objection to the taking of marine and sea-bird life, except for food, and in the above case I felt the poor brute had appealed to us for rest and protection. Speaking of killing marine life I mean with the exception of the Shark, which like all sailors I try to kill on sight, and it is a saying at sea, that the only good Shark is a dead one.

We arrived at San Francisco in due course, and after lying there for about two months, we went to a place called Port Costa, to load Wheat for Europe, calling at Queenstown for orders. After loading, we came back to San Francisco to pick up a crew, but as men were scarce, and ships wanting crews plentiful, it took me 14 days to secure one.

There was great competition among the Captains looking for crews, and many amusing incidents occurred, but before I relate the following yarn, I must tell you we were paying 90 Gold Dollars (£18) and two months advance per head for every man we got. That is, we paid the money to the person who secured us the man. Of course it was crimping [press-ganging] pure and simple, and I must admit we were not over particular as to ways and means. It happened one day that a friendly Captain and I were standing in the street comparing notes, and bemoaning our hard luck, when a man came up to us and said, "Do either of you want a sailor?"

"Yes," we both answered. "Have you one, and where is he?"

"In jail," was the answer, "but I can get him out if it is good enough," meaning of course, the money. Now I had my eyes on two or three men that no-one else knew about, and wanting to get my friend out of the way, I made a virtue of necessity, and said, "All right old man, you take him," so he went to look the man up. The crimp took him to the Police Court, and as in America all magistrates are addressed as Judge, the man walked my friend up to the Judge's seat, and introduced him as follows, "Say, Judge, this is the Captain of an English ship and is willing to take for a sailer Jack so-and-so, who you committed to the House of Detention as a vagrant."

The Judge, without the slightest change of demeanour leaned aside to the crimp and said, "How much is there in it for me?"

"25 dollars," was the answer.

"Right," said the Judge, and then ordered the Police to put the man in custody on board. Sharp work for the Land of Freedom. In the meantime I shipped four men which completed my crew. My friend also managed to complete his, and we arranged to sail next morning. At midnight I was sitting reading in my room, with two shore watchmen with loaded revolvers patrolling the deck to prevent crimps boarding us and stealing the crew. I suddenly heard a great commotion in the Harbour— men shouting and whistles blowing. We could not make head or tail of it, but surmised that someone was in the water. However on arrival home I met my friend, the Captain above mentioned, and he told me his jail bird had jumped overboard, and was last seen striking out for the shore. It was not known if he got there, but the ship had to go without him. Next morning we started in tow for sea, and just before approaching close to the shore at the entrance of the Golden Gate, I ordered the quarter boat to be swung in and lashed. No sooner was this done than the cry of "Man overboard" was heard, and it took some time before the boat was got into the water, but I saw the man striking out for the shore all he knew how, and I knew what he was up to at once. He reached the shore before the boat did, and the second officer who was in the boat reported that the man was surrounded by a crowd of roughs, who dared the boat's crew to come and take the man. The officer thought discretion the better part of valour, and he was quite right, but all the same bang went £26. Verily, the way of transgressors is hard, but who was the transgressor in this case?

Well, on the passage home we had the usual run of gales and calms, but arrived safely at Queenstown, and received orders to go to Dunkirk, my wife, son, and youngest daughter joining me there. From Dunkirk we went to Cardiff, my wife this time going round in the ship. On arrival I got the ship's business into shape, and we then went to Liverpool, principally for the sake of me seeing our new home, my wife having removed to Brook Road, Bootle, during my absence on the last voyage. I was only in Liverpool a few days, and then returned to Cardiff with all the family, Minnie Mitchell included.

On October the 17th 1888, I sailed for Rangoon, arriving there February 3rd 1889, sailing thence with a cargo of Rice to Rio de Janeiro, arriving there May 24th 1889, thus making the passage in 74 days—the quickest on record. The pleasure of the passage was greatly marred by the loss of one of my apprentices, who fell from aloft when off the Cape of Good Hope, and was killed. The Cook also died of blood-poisoning, and further I had to leave my second officer in hospital at Rio, he suffering from Pneumonia.

We left Rio on the 27th June for New York, arriving there August 3rd 1889. My wife and youngest daughter joined me there, coming from Liverpool in the S.S. Alaska, the then quickest liner afloat, but soon to be eclipsed by others.

# Chapter 6

*1889 A close shave—last voyage on a sailing ship—
a ship's boat discovered—the ruins of Ayuthia in Siam—
negotiations*

We spent quite a pleasant time in New York, and my cousin, W. J. Bryson, came from Chicago to see us. In the meantime my wife heard from an Uncle and Aunt Stephen in Norfolk, Virginia. They pressed her very much to come and see them, and it was finally arranged that she should go to them when I sailed. We were then loading a cargo of Case Oil for Bangkok, Siam, so after arranging for my wife's passage home in one of the White Star steamers (the Germanic) I saw her into the train on the morning of the 19th September, and received a wire that evening telling of her safe arrival at Norfolk, where she stayed some three weeks, then returning home. On Friday, 20th September 1889, I sailed on what proved to be my last voyage in a sailing ship. The then Chief Officer had been with me for some years, and was a much older man than myself—a good soul, but very superstitious, and when he heard we were to sail on Friday, he begged me not to do so, and went so far as to appeal to my wife to use her influence with me to prevent the Friday sailing, telling her something was sure to happen if we sailed on that day. I was very much annoyed with him for upsetting my wife, and like all obstinate men, I made every effort to get away on that day.

We left New York on a beautiful fine day, and discharged the tug and pilot off Sandy Hook, the pilot saying as he left, "You are having a good start Captain, and the weather is very fine," so we made all plain sail, but within an hour after doing so, a gale of wind burst on us like a clap of thunder. Quick as the wind came I gave orders to shorten sail, and soon had her under reefed topsails and foresail. The second officer—an old apprentice of mine—told me afterwards that the mate was giving his orders in the following fashion, "Haul in the weather main top-gallant brace"—"This comes of sailing on a Friday"—"Belay the weather clewline"—"Damn young fool, I told him so"—"Jump round lively men"—"Serve him damn well right if he loses her"—and so on.

Well, I must say I came very nearly losing her that night. We were going along under three reefed topsails, foresails, jib, and lower staysails, the wind well on the starboard beam, and ship making good headway. About 3 o'clock in the morning, I concluded I was well clear of a nest of rocks called 'Mathews Vineyard' [Martha's Vineyard] down to leeward of me, so I went on deck, and kept her off two points and squared in the yards, but after I had done so I became very uneasy, and had a strong premonition that I was running into danger, something seemed to be telling me without ceasing, "Brace the yards up and haul her to the wind."

So strongly was I impressed with the warning, that within half on hour after the last alteration of trim, I gave the order to brace up and keep to seaward. At 6 a.m. the day broke, and to my dismay I found we were in the vicinity of the rocks. Fortunately, the wind was hauling more to the Westward, and I was able to haul off. None but myself knew how close we were to these hidden dangers and to destruction, though the mate did remark that we seemed to be in a tide race.

I said, "Yes, it looks like it." Nevertheless, after we were in safety, I went to my room and thanked God with all my heart for His guidance and mercy.

Before proceeding further with my story, I want my readers to understand that I am not—and never was—a believer in the old sailors' superstition that it was unlucky to sail on Friday, and I have only told the foregoing story to show how ordinary happenings may confirm a superstitious person in their beliefs.

While I am still close to the subject of personal warnings, I will relate a remarkable story of the sea as told to me by an eye-witness. The narrator of the story was at one time second mate with me, but at the time of the event he was second mate on a vessel homeward bound from a port on the West Coast of North America. When in the North Pacific, his ship was going along about four knots an hour on a fine day, the Captain, his wife, and little girl were sitting on the poop deck, when the child (then about seven years old) suddenly jumped up and said, "Oh, papa, I see a boat." The father looking round, and not seeing anything, scolded the child, who persisted in saying she saw a boat, at the same time pointing to leeward. The father was very angry with the child, and told the mother she must punish her if she persisted in telling falsehoods, but the mother knowing the child was truthful, tried to sooth the sobbing little one, who still maintained she could see the boat. The mother then suggested that someone should go aloft, and have a good look round. A man was sent up, and saw nothing until he reached the main royal yard, and then he reported a small object on the lee beam. The ship was at once kept away, and on reaching the object, it proved to be a ship's boat, with several men, and one woman, all lying as dead, except the woman, who could just speak. They were the Captain, his wife, and part of the crew of a vessel which had foundered, and were at their last gasp for want of water, and the reason the woman had the most life was that the men had stinted themselves to give her more. At the time the child saw the boat, the lady was praying fervently to God for deliverance. I know the story is true, because I heard of the rescue before from other sources, but I did not know the part the child took in it. If this rescue was not a direct answer to prayer, then who opened the eyes of the little child, when the eyes of the experienced sailors were closed?

Resuming my story I may say our voyage was fairly uneventful, until we reached the Java and China sea, and then we got it hot and strong in the way of bad weather. I have been a great deal in the Java and China Seas, but I have never experienced anything like the weather we got on this passage—that is, for this part of the world. On Christmas morning, when to the North-East of Natuna Islands, a gale burst upon us without warning, blowing away all our sails, and from that day until New Year's Day (1890) it blew a constant heavy gale from West, raining, with thunder and lightning all the time, but with the New Year the wind moderated and hauled to North and N.E., and we bore away for the Gulf of Siam, arriving off Bangkok Bar on the 8th January 1890, making a passage of 109 days from New York, the quickest passage between the two ports ever recorded. We commenced discharging, and continued until the ship was light enough to cross the Bar, when we towed up to a position three miles below Bangkok, and made the ship fast to the Coconut trees on the River Bank—a new experience for me in the way of Coconuts and Mosquitoes, the latter coming off in such swarms, that one could not draw a sudden breath without sucking some into the mouth. Fortunately, they were not so venomous as some I have seen, but as it was, my crew were nearly driven frantic, and they had to go on shore and build wood fires so that the smoke would drive off the pests, but which was the most disagreeable, the smoke or the mosquitoes, I really cannot say. I slept in my room through it all, but then I was always a hard case where mosquitoes are concerned.

After lying at Bangkok for nearly two months, I received a wire from my owners to proceed to Saigon to load. I promptly wired back, "Ballast not procurable, can offer you so much for loading here." For three days I had no reply, and then I got a cable to proceed to Rangoon. Now, if I could not get ballast for one port, I could not get it for another, so I was in a bit of a fix, and I fear I said some very naughty words regarding the common sense of my owners. They were exceedingly nice people, but were very prone to strain at a gnat and swallow a camel where freights were concerned.

However, I set to work to see what could be done, but not a pound of ballast was to be had in Bangkok. After a day or two had passed, I heard that at a place called Ayuthia (the ancient capital of Siam, then in ruins) there were mounds of rubbish and earth which would be easily secured, but the place was situated some 70 miles up the River, and the question was how to get there. I overcame the difficulty by chartering a small steamer, took Command of her, and started off to see what could be done, only to find that no-one had power to grant me permission to remove the earth, nor would the officials grant such permission without the consent of the King, whose property it was, so I had to come back empty-handed. Nevertheless, I enjoyed the trip to Ayuthia, seeing there the ruins of the old Palace, and also the Elephant traps for which the place is famous.

On my return to Bangkok, I heard that on the Island of Kosichang, some 15 miles from Bangkok Bar, there was a large shingle beach, and a good harbour, so I saw the Governor of the Province—Prince Samuti— and asked his permission to take what I wanted of the shingle. He of course—Asiatic-like—saw his way to make money, and on my telling him I wanted 500 tons, he said I might take that quantity for 1,000 dollars. This was equal to 7/6 per ton, and of course I would have to defray all other expenses. Now I had a strong objection to being squeezed, and told him I was not prepared to buy the Island, but only wanted to take the sand and shingle off the beach, and after offering him 500 dollars—which he would not take—I said we had better leave the matter open until I had seen what facilities the place afforded. Now, Kosichang is a good-sized Island, with only a few fishermen for inhabitants, but the King had a summer house and an hotel there, some of the European residents of Bangkok using the latter as a Sanatorium, and a large steam launch ran daily from Bangkok. I may also add that vessels went there to load when there was too much sea at the Bar for lighters to lie alongside.

To cut my story short, I again engaged the small steamer, and went to Kosichang, hoping to find there the solution of the ballast problem, but I was again disappointed. There was however an Italian barque in the Harbour, and thinking she might have ballast which her Master would be prepared to dispose of, I went on board, and found I was just too late, he having thrown his spare ballast overboard preparatory to loading timber, but I found the beginning of the end on board, in the shape of an Italian resident of Bangkok, who told me that his friend, Mr Grassie, had a contract with the King of Siam to pull down some old buildings within the Palace grounds, and they were also excavating for new foundations. This was indeed good news, so after thanking him for the information, I got back to Bangkok as fast as possible, and interviewed the Contractor, making a bargain to take as much as I wanted for 500 dollars, he assuring me that his agreement with the King gave him the right to dispose of the stuff in any way he chose.

With the foregoing agreement made, I thought my troubles were ended, but I soon found they were only beginning. The Contractor drove me over to the location, which I found was two miles up a Creek which had very little water in it, so I had to engage small boats to take the ballast out to large launches, which after being loaded we towed to the ship. After sufficient had been put in the ship to keep her upright, I had to tow her to Kosichang, there being only 13 ft. 6 ins. of water on the Bar. While engaged in taking the ship out, I left the Chinese Contractor to load up 350 tons of ballast into launches. Having seen the ship safely anchored at Kosichang, I hurried back to superintend the shipping of the ballast, but on arrival I found all work stopped, the Chinese contractor telling me the Siamese soldiers had threatened to shoot them if they took any more.

This story took me all aback, and nearly threw me on my beam-ends, so I sat down under a tree and indulged in a few sailor-like remarks, which included Siamese, Chinese, and their respective manners and customs. Thus easing my mind, I went to hunt up my Italian friend, and with him went at once to see the Minister of War, a real live Prince, who I found could talk English very well. After stating my case, he coolly told me that there was a large heap of earth in the Court Yard of the War Office, which he required taking away, and that he had ordered the Chinese Contractor to work on, but the man not obeying, he ordered the soldiers to prevent him doing any more until he obeyed. I respectfully but firmly pointed out that to carry out his orders would cost double what I was paying the Chinese Contractor, but if he would pay the extra cost, I was quite willing to oblige him. After some further discussion, he withdrew his veto, and my work began again, but on the following morning all work was again stopped for the same reason as before, so again I hunted up my Italian friend, and interviewed the Prince, who told me I was in Siam, and he intended to have his orders obeyed, and that he did not propose to have any Chinaman disobey him.

To this I replied as follows, "Your Highness is quite right, we are in Siam, but you have overlooked the fact that I bought the stuff from Mr Grassie, not from the Siamese Government, and I am also aware that a Treaty exists between your country and mine, which gives British subjects a right to engage in all manner of lawful trade in Siam, and as my agreement with Mr Grassie, and his with your Government, are lawful contracts, I must respectfully tell you that if you don't allow my work to go on unmolested, I will place my case in the hands of the British Minister."

This seemed to amuse the gentleman, for he laughed and said, "You know too much, Captain, but you might remove my stuff all the same."

I replied, "With pleasure, if your Highness will pay the extra cost."

However, I got my way, loaded the larchers and sent them to Kosichang. After settling up my business, I bid Good-bye to Bangkok, went down to my ship and found all going on well.

I may mention that on my reaching my ship I found a Hong Kong steamer lying close to, and learned that my brother-in-law, James Mitchell (Minnie's father) was Chief Officer of her, and I may also add that my Chief Officer, Mr Follett—of Friday sailing fame—heard from a brother, who was master of a Singapore steamer. He offered his brother a berth as Chief, with promise of Command, so I let him go, the brother sending me a new Chief from Singapore.

I left Kosichang on the 21st March, and arrived at Rangoon on the 1st May 1890, loaded a cargo of Rice, and sailed at the end of the month for Liverpool, having had to call in at St. Helena on the way home to land my Chief Officer, who was very far gone in consumption, the poor fellow dying about a week after he was landed.

We arrived in Liverpool on the 16th September, and docked in the East Waterloo Dock, after an absence from home of two years.

In concluding this chapter I may add that quite unexpectedly this proved to be my last voyage in sailing ships—after being in them for 25 years. I left them with much regret at the time, for I never had any desire to go into steam, but times were altering, and the days of sailing ships were numbered, 'Ichabod' being written large over their roll of fame [inglorious son, from book of Samuel]. Further, I had a wife and family to keep, so like the rats I deserted the sinking ship, much to the benefit of myself and those depending on me. How this change came about I will relate in a future chapter, but I will tell my readers that the foregoing narrative is but a brief account of what I have seen and experienced. I can tell yarns of my life by the hour, but writing was never my strong point, so the yarns, like the sailing vessel, must die a natural death.

# Chapter 7

*1890 The coming of steam—taken on by Messrs. Alfred Holt & Co—Chief Officer, then full Command*

I will now give the reasons, and relate some of the incidents, which caused me to give up sailing ships and go into steamers.

I was always proud of being a sailing-ship sailor, notwithstanding its attendant hardships, and looked with scorn on the young men who joined steamers early in life, and considered that they to some extent had 'swallowed the anchor', and given up because the life was too hard for them. I still think so of the men I speak of, but we are nearly all steamboat sailors now, because the days of sailing ships are over, and it was the knowledge that their days were passing away that caused me to accept the change when it was offered to me. Further, I had a grievance regarding my pay as Master of the Morna, not having had an increase during the ten years I was Master of her, though it was promised, "If times got better," but they never did, and no matter how good freights were, I was always put off with nice little pats on the back, and so forth, so I was about tired of looking forward to the 'milk and honey' which never came.

I had been home about two weeks, and was preparing the Morna to load Salt for Calcutta, when I received a note from Captain W. Ray, asking me to come and see him. On my doing so, he said, "I don't think the people you are with have treated you well in the matter of salary. Now I have an offer to make you, which from some points of view, is a good one. I have been empowered to appoint a Master to the ship Windsor Park, the pay is much better than you are getting, and you can take your family with you, but," he said, "the owners have only one ship, and if times get worse, they may sell her, and then you will be in a bad fix. On the other hand, your own people will not in the course of nature last long, so there you are again. Have you never thought of going into steam?"

I answered, "No, but if anyone will offer me Command, I will go."

"No doubt you would," he replied, "but in the meantime, go and talk Windsor Park to the wife and give me an answer in a day or two."

That same evening, while discussing the proposed change with the wife, my brother Edward came in, and said, "Our people (Messrs. Holt) would like to see you, and want you to call tomorrow."

I said, "What for?"

He answered, "Go and see" and would say nothing more.

So because he would not speak plainer, I, in my pigheadedness said, "Your people can go to Jerusalem, I don't want to see them."

"Well," he said, "will you go for my sake? It may do me good."

So I said, "Certainly," and went next day.

On my going to Messrs. Holt's office, I saw Mr

Crompton, the then manager, and also Captain Russell, the firm's Nautical Adviser, After some small talk, Mr Crompton said, "We understand, Captain, that you wish to go into steam."

Now this was a surprise to me, and I came very nearly to saying, "I don't." But prudence prevailed and I said, "Yes, but it entirely depends upon what is offered me."

"What are you looking for?" he said, "and what do you expect?"

I answered, "I am looking for Command."

"Oh, that is out of the question," he replied. "You see, we have as second officers with us, men who have been in command of steamers."

"That may be, Sir," I replied, "but perhaps they were in want of employment. I am not, and further I am 40 years of age, and have been Master too long to voluntarily undertake to play second fiddle again. What I want is to go forward, not backward, and the sacrifice in time and money which would necessarily follow my taking an officer's berth, is too great for me to undertake, but may I ask what you intended to offer me?"

After a few minutes thought, he said, "Would you mind waiting for a few minutes, Captain, while I consult with the firm."

He and Captain Russell then retired, leaving me to my thoughts, which were rather mixed, but in the ten minutes or so that I was alone, my resolution was strengthened, and I made up my mind to accept nothing less than Command. When Mr Crompton returned, I was quite cool and ready for him. For a few seconds neither of us spoke, but looked each other steadily in the eyes.

He broke the silence by asking, "Are you a teetotaller, Captain?"

"No," I said, "I am not but I am a very moderate man—indeed, so moderate that I rarely touch anything in the way of liquor."

"I am glad to hear you say that," he replied, "for we don't want our people to be teetotallers. Now I will make you an offer, which is a good one, but first let me remind you that you have never been in steam, and you don't know the routine of our business, so if I offer you a Chief Officer's berth for one, or at the most, two voyages, with a definite promise of Command afterwards, I think you will see that is the most I can offer consistent with the Company's interests."

"Sir," I replied, "I thank you for the offer, which I recognise as a good one, but no doubt you will understand my reluctance to accept it off hand, and I would like to talk the matter over with my wife before deciding." I then told him of Captain Ray's offer, and after some further talk, Mr Crompton said, "Let me advise you to accept our offer. Think it over carefully, and give me your answer one week from today."

On arriving home that evening, I found the whole family gathered to hear the news. When I told them of the offer, they all—wife, brother, niece, and children—exclaimed, "Of course, you have accepted it."

In reply I answered, "No, I have not, nor do I feel inclined to do so."

My brother was very much upset on hearing this, and after some talk he said, "Jack, I never thought you were a fool, Good night," and off he went, my wife going with him to the door, and as they had a long confab, I knew he was asking her to use all her influence to make me accept the offer.

When alone with my wife I asked her to give me her views on the situation, and without hesitation she said, "It is my earnest desire that you take Messrs. Holt's offer. Look at the long weary voyages you have been making, and at the children growing up and hardly ever seeing their Father, besides look at the anxiety for me, dreading every wind that blows, hoping for the best and dreading the worst, until my nerves are all upset", and then she began to cry. By all the rules of married life, that ought to have settled it, but I fancied that the question required further thought, so I soothed the little wife as best I could, and hung on to my pride and foolishness like a sailor to a Jackstay.

Having made up my mind to accept one of the two offers made me I thought it only right that I should inform my employers—Messrs. J.H. Worthington & Co—of my intention. On my doing so, they were much surprised, and expressed great regret at my thinking of leaving them.

Now I will confess that I was quite undecided as to which offer I was going to accept, and when the day came on which I had to give an answer, I left home in the morning not knowing what I intended to do. On my way to town I came to the conclusion to see Captain Ray first, and on doing so explained my position and gave my reasons for hesitating in both cases.

After I had finished speaking, he looked at me and said, "John Goodwin, I have known you for a long time, but I never had reason to think that you could be such a damn fool as to hesitate over such an offer as Holt's have made you. Go at once and accept it." Well, I took his advice, resigned Command of the Morna, was appointed Chief Officer of the S.S. Cyclops—Captain H. Nish—and joined her on Monday the 11th October 1890, the ship then lying in the Morpeth Dock, Birkenhead. And I must confess I was anything but reconciled to the change I had made and for the week in dock before sailing, I kept calling myself several kinds of fool for making the change. However, we sailed on the 18th October for Algiers, Port Said, Penang, Singapore, Hong Kong, and Shanghai, having on board some 20 passengers for China.

As we steamed down the River, we passed my old ship, the Morna, towing to sea, outward bound to Calcutta. It made me very sad to think that I had left her, but I soon got over that, and I may mention that I did not see the Morna again until six years had passed, she by that time having been sold to the Norwegians. 'Ichabod' was written large all over her and I could only sigh and say, "Alas! how are the mighty fallen." I have never seen her since, nor have I heard what became of her.

I soon accustomed myself to my new position, and got along very well with the Captain. I suppose I must have given him satisfaction, though I know he did not relish having a man who was an older shipmaster than himself as Chief Officer.

I was very much amused two or three days after leaving by the Captain telling me to bend the square foresail and set it, he very carefully telling me how it was to be done. I kept my face quite straight and said, "Aye, aye, Sir," and carried out his orders, but the same evening the wind hauled abeam and he told me to set the jib and proceeded to describe minutely how it was to be done. This was too much for me, and I just looked at him and laughed. He saw the point at once, and responded with, "Oh, go and set it your own damn way," and when I got back on the bridge, he said, "I forgot you know a darn sight more about setting sails than I do."

Well, we made the voyage in good shape, arriving in London on the 10th February 1891, proceeding from there to Glasgow to load a general cargo for Java, finishing loading at Liverpool and sailing on the 14th March 1891 for Batavia [Jakarta, Indonesia] via Algiers and Singapore. I don't know that there is much to remark upon as far as the voyage is concerned, but on completion of the voyage I considered that I had performed my part of the contract and I called on Mr Crompton and told him so. He was very nice, but sorry he had nothing for me just then, the new ships then building not being up to time, and he finished up by saying, "You don't mind going another voyage as mate?"

As a matter of fact I did, but there was no help for it, so I smiled and looked as pleasant as I could.

On the following day I got a note appointing me to relieve Captain Nish as Master of the Cyclops on the passage from London to Glasgow and Liverpool.

# Chapter 8

I joined the S.S. Cyclops in London, took her round to Glasgow and had one of the worst passages for weather I have ever experienced in Channel, but got her to Glasgow safely, loaded a part cargo for China, and then took the ship to Liverpool, and thus ended my first Command in steam. Much to my disappointment the Command was not made permanent, and I had to go back to Chief Officer for another voyage. This, although very annoying, was for my good, for on this voyage we carried Mahometan Pilgrims from Singapore and Penang to Jeddah—a thing I had never done before. On leaving Penang we had 1,300 men, women and children on board, and called first at a place on the Arabian Coast in the Red Sea, called Kamaran. There we landed all the Pilgrims for five days Quarantine, and during that time we cleaned and disinfected the ship, then re-embarked the Pilgrims, proceeded to Jeddah and landed them there. The foregoing job was a very interesting one, but very dirty, and we had 17 deaths among the Pilgrims, and nearly all our crew were more or less sick with a bad form of Diarrhoea, but I gained a great deal of experience and some knowledge of the two Ports—Kamaran and Jeddah—both of which are bad Ports to make, on account of the reefs which surround the entrances, and as some of the Company's ships go there every year, it was well for me to see the places before taking all the responsibilities.

The things to be dreaded in carrying these Pilgrims are outbreaks of Smallpox and Cholera, and during the last few years Plague has been added to the risks we have to run, so it will be quite understood when I say that none of the men in the ship are in love with the job, and are all very thankful when we get the Pilgrims out of the ship. However, nowadays we have plenty of good water on board, and this goes a long way towards keeping people in good health.

Speaking of water and its effect on health, I may mention an experience of my own, which might be quoted to prove that indifferent water was really good for the health. This occurred while the ship Morna—which I then commanded—was lying in the Bangkok River. Now at that time Bangkok had no water supply other than the River, which from two hours before, to two hours after high water, was brackish, and unfit to drink. Further, all the filth and sewage from the town went into the River, and along the Banks the Siamese natives built their houses on poles carried down to low water mark. In the floors of their houses a sort of trap door was cut, and through this all the sewage and filth was thrown into the River, and all drinking water was drawn up by buckets, so my readers can imagine what a nice sanitary condition prevailed.

Now the Morna was lying just far enough below the town to have only one hour each side of low water, in which water could be got fresh enough for use, but this was about the time the worst of the sewage was abreast of us going and returning, and the water was as thick as, and the colour of, pea soup, but as no other was to be had, and beggars cannot be choosers, we had to make the best of it, so I caused two big ton casks to be placed on end on the deck, and the upper heads taken out, letting cocks into the lower part of the casks, about a foot from the bottom end. We filled these casks every day, sprinkled alum on the top of the water, let them stand for about 20 hours, and then ran the water into our tanks, scrubbing out the casks and repeating every low water. My crew and self drank this water for four months, and not one of us was sick, but on arrival at Rangoon we got what was considered to be good water, and all hands but myself got bad Diarrhoea. Now I will make no remarks on the subject, but leave my readers to read, mark, learn, and inwardly digest the foregoing narrative, and draw their own conclusions.

Resuming my story, I may say we made the last mentioned voyage successfully, and arrived home about the beginning of June 1892. I then saw Mr Crompton, the Company's Manager, and after some talk he pointed out that there was no vacancy at the moment, but that there would be one in about three months, and if I chose to stay back on my own account—which of course meant without pay—I would get the appointment. I did not think I was being treated fairly or that he was carrying out the promises made me on joining the Company, but I had to grin and bear it, like many a better man before me. Nevertheless I was glad of the holiday, as it would give me the longest time I ever had with my family, but it meant a lot out of pocket. That did not worry me much but I did not think I was being treated in a straight-forward manner. However, when I had been home about six weeks, I was sent for, and appointed Master of the Hector, 1,350 tons Register, sailing under the Dutch flag, in the Java trade. There is an old saying that a man with a double crown on his head will serve under two flags. Well, I have a double crown, and have thus fulfilled the prophesy.

The Hector was lying in London when I joined her, in the latter part of July 1892, and having partly loaded we went over to Amsterdam to complete our loading for Singapore and Java ports. My wife was with me in London, but as Cholera was very bad on the Continent, I sent her home from London. We both felt it hard, as I was to be a fortnight in Amsterdam, but I dare not risk taking her, as she was at that time subject to bad attacks of Diarrhoea, so we had to make one more of those sacrifices which sailors and their wives are so often called upon to make. I sailed away from Amsterdam at the end of August 1892, looking forward to the home-coming and meeting my dear wife again.

On my appointment to the Hector the Manager told me the Company wished to inaugurate a new procedure with regard to the route, and the number of times called at each port, and so save time and money. To enable this to be done, he instructed me to proceed to London and take sole charge of the loading, giving me a free hand in all respects. I am glad to say I was able to carry out the Company's wishes to the letter, and thus justified my appointment, and it was the more to my credit, owing to the fact that all parties concerned were of opinion that it could not be done satisfactorily. Even the Manager doubted, and told me so.

Well, to be brief, I made four voyages to Java in the Hector, carrying Dutch cabin passengers each voyage. On the fourth voyage homewards, I completed loading at the Port of Cochin on the West Coast of India—a very interesting and old-fashioned place. I have never seen it since, and probably never will again. We arrived at Amsterdam on the 12th October 1892, having experienced very bad weather in Channel. From Amsterdam we proceeded to London, and I went down to Liverpool for a few days, returning to London on the 25th October for the purpose of bringing my ship to Liverpool, arriving there on the 29th October. We had bad weather round the Coast, and I had long spells on the bridge, and must have caught a chill, for on arrival home my wife said, "How flushed you are," and putting her hand on my head she exclaimed, "Why you are burning hot."

Well, I put my feet in hot water and mustard, took a glass of hot whisky and water, and got to bed, and had a good sweat, and in the morning I felt as fit as a well-loaded ship in a seaway.

On going down to the office the Manager congratulated me on looking so well, and on escaping the Java fever. I am afraid I felt what may be termed 'cocky'—swelled-head we call it nowadays—forgetting that a man should not boast himself of his strength, also that our Saviour had said, "Let him that thinketh he standeth take heed lest he fall."

Now during the last voyage I had grown very stout indeed. I felt bloated and my dear wife said I looked it, and that she would far rather have me the bag of bones and sinew of my younger days than as I was then. I had also been troubled with suppressed pains in my limbs and muscles, but it never occurred to me that my constitution was fighting the Fever which had introduced itself into my system. However on the third day after my arrival home, I felt very unwell, and about noon while sitting by the fire, I felt the deadly chill of Malaria come over me, so saying to my wife, "I have the Java fever and am off to bed", I directed her as to what she should do, and promptly had a good smart attack.

This was on the 2nd November 1893, and I did not come out of the bedroom until January 1st 1894, and after that had to go to bed again, and did not get about until about the 21st January. I had a bad time of it and I think the Malaria played every trick it knew, for I had it stationary, progressive, and retrogressive, but thanks to a good constitution, my dear wife's nursing, and the treatment of the best Homoeopathic Doctor (Dr Peter Stuart, Rodney Street) in Liverpool, and above all, God's great goodness and mercy I recovered, but Malaria never leaves a man entirely, and it took two years before I ceased having attacks, and then I had a space of about five years free, but since then if I take a chill, I get an attack, which lasts about 36 hours, and then I feel quite well again.

Now it will be quite understood that having this illness, I had to give up my ship, and of course this worried me a good deal, but my employers behaved very well, sending up and telling me not to worry as I should have another ship when better, and that during my illness they would pay me £20 sterling per month. For this and other things I had a great deal to be thankful for. Amongst other things I learned what a loving unselfish woman my dear wife was, and also what a sweet-natured child my youngest daughter Bessie was [born 1886]. She and I were drawn together in bonds of love and affection at that time, a connection which has lasted until this day, though she has grown into womanhood, but while speaking of her I may describe her for the benefit of those who may come after, that is, if these lines ever reach the hands of my children's children, which I trust they will, for it is for that object I have taken the trouble to write them.

Mary Elizabeth Williamson Goodwin—commonly called 'Bessie'—is a tall graceful girl, about 5 ft. 7 inches in height, has fair hair, and a small sweet face, an index to an unselfish loving nature, yet she has force of character, and a determination to succeed in her undertakings, is a good speaker, a lady in every respect, and a fairly healthy, sweet English maiden. I dare say some of my readers will say, "Oh, a foolish father, writing of his duckling as a swan." Not so, for thanks to the good sense of her mother and sisters, she has not been spoiled in any way. I certainly had no chance to spoil her, and would not if I could.

Now I think it is time I told a yarn to relieve the dullness of this chapter, so I will take up the slack of my jaw tackles, ease off my boom sheets, and reel off a few ghost stories. So my dear descendants, close the door tight, see all the lights are burning, and gather round the reader, and listen to your Grandfather's yarns.

In the early part of my narrative, I mentioned that for nine years my family lived in a house in Bootle, that if not haunted came precious near being so. It was a three-storied house above the street, with basement kitchens half below the street in front, and level with the garden at the back. Above the top floor landing there was a trap door in the ceiling, leading to the eaves of the house. It was never used because there were no steps leading up to it, and we found out there was no connection between the two next houses, so that no-one could gain access to our place in that way. Moreover the trap was quite nine feet from the floor. My wife told me that often in the middle of the night she would hear footsteps coming down the stairs, often they would stop at her door and then pass on. At other times the catch of the door would be turned and the door placed ajar, the footsteps then returning, but after this had continued for a good time, the ghost—or whatever it was—got bolder, and used to open the door and walk into the room. My wife used to keep the gas burning low all night, yet she never saw anything, but had an uncomfortable feeling of some presence. She was brave enough to turn on the gas full at times, so it cannot be said that what she heard was the fancy of a nervous woman, and to prove this was not so, I relate the following stories.

About the beginning of February 1894, I was convalescent from the Fever, and the Doctor wished me to go higher up the town for a week—that is, to a higher situation than my own house—so my wife and I went to stay with our brother-in-law—Mr Parry—for a week, leaving our house in charge of my eldest daughter, the other children and servant also being there. About the third morning after leaving home, my daughter Carrie came up and told her mother that each night since we left home, she had been awakened out of her sleep by footsteps coming down stairs in no gentle manner. She awakened her sister, who slept with her, and both heard the footsteps. On the night previous to coming to tell us, they were so terrified that they determined to stand it no longer, but before coming to us they mustered all hands for a search in the upper rooms, when to their amazement they found the cover for the trap in the ceiling had been partly taken off. That was quite enough for them, so Carrie hurried off to us.

Our nephew—Tom Parry—a sea officer, was then at home, so he went down immediately, got a ladder fixed, and went into the eaves, but could find no means of exit, so he drove a strong staple into the cover of the trap, which was about three feet long, by two feet wide, placed a bearer under the coamings, and lashed it down tight. He slept in the house that night, and no sound was heard, but in the morning they found the trap cover had been moved from the following position:

 to this:

So Tom got another staple and lashed the cover as follows:

after which this particular manifestation ceased, but worse followed, for the ghost began to materialize and turned its attention to the wife [now returned home], who often when sitting in a room alone at evening time, would hear a deep sigh uttered close to her. Of course she never stood on the order of her going, but got out like a streak of lightning, so the ghost giving her up in despair began to pay court to Meg—my second daughter. Her first experience was under the following circumstances.

The young folk had two or three friends in the house one evening to keep them company, their mother having gone to her sister's house. The servant girl being also out, the young ones were all in the dining room, and during the course of the evening they found there was no coal upstairs, and as none of them would go down stairs alone, all hands—amongst whom there were two boys of 16 and my own son of 14—went down to the coal vault. One of the young fellows took the coal box and opened the cellar door for her. On the door being opened, a dark object like a big monkey pushed against Meg, and rushed across the kitchen into a corner and glared at them. They all saw it, but a moment or two was enough for them, then they fled upstairs. Afterwards when describing what they had seen, all agreed it was a dwarf or monkey.

A week or two after the foregoing adventure, my wife was alone in the house, and coal was wanted, so without thinking, she took up the coal box and sailed down stairs to the coal vault. Facing the coal in the vault, she had the door on her left hand, and a blank wall on her right. Stooping to get coal she leaned towards the wall, when to her horror, a living tangible presence pushed past her. Well, the dear little woman who had sailed calmly down stairs under low canvas, flew up with every stitch set, and did not stir tack nor sheet until she came to an anchor in the dining room.

Shortly, after the last happening, Meg was in the bathroom, and my wife and Carrie in the dining room, when, they heard a sharp blow struck on the bathroom door, and Meg called out, "Now then Carrie, don't you be trying to frighten me."

Carrie had the good sense to go to the stairs and call out, "All right, Meg," but she had hardly returned to the room before bang it went again, and Meg called out in a frightened voice, "Mother, Carrie," so of course they rushed upstairs, and found nothing to account for the noise, but Meg declared that before each blow on the door her name was whispered through the keyhole.

Several times after this, when Meg was in the bathroom in the evening, something would keep pulling at the bottom of her skirts, so at last she could not go there alone. When I was told of this, I confess I had my doubts, and thought it was nervousness on her part, but one evening a young girl friend of ours was in the bathroom washing her hands, the door open and my two daughters were in the next room, when they heard a frightened voice calling out, "Girls, girls," so they ran to her, and found her almost in a fainting condition. On calming down she told them that something was pulling at her skirts in short quick jerks, so they told her it must be fancy or a mouse. Now this young girl knew nothing of our ghost, as Mother had told her girls not to talk about it, and so my doubts with regard to Meg's story were dispelled.

I will relate one or two more happenings, and then have done with ghosts.

In the latter part of the year 1896, one evening my wife and two daughters were sitting in the dining room, when Meg got up and ran upstairs singing as she went. Suddenly they heard her shriek and running up they found her lying on her bed in Hysterics. On coming round she told her mother that on reaching the first landing a man stepped out right before her. She dodged him and ran to her room, and fell fainting on the bed. Of course they searched the house but found nothing.

In the early part of the year 1893, my two daughters and a dressmaker were sitting in the top front room sewing, time about 11 a.m. The mother was out shopping, taking her latch key with her, as she was without a servant for the time being. The three persons in the room were talking together quite happily, when they heard someone coming upstairs, stopping finally at the room door. The handle of the latter was turned and Carrie called out, "Now mother, don't be playing tricks, but open the door and come in." The door was immediately opened, but no-one came in. Of course they were very much frightened and ran downstairs, finding all fast below and Mother still out. Well, this about finished them, and when I came home from New York in April, we took another house and moved, but of this later on.

I cannot resist telling just one more story, though I was not directly interested in it. A Chief Officer I had with me in 1904/5—a cool-headed man—who when home lived in Clifton, near Bristol, and owned the house they lived in, which was a large one. His mother and sister kept house, he not being married. Now, two or three servants, one after another, gave notice to leave, saying the house was haunted by a woman whom they had seen. Shortly after the third girl had left, the sister met in the hall a woman in a Nurse's dress, with a Sister's cap on her head. She was very much startled, but said, "What do you want?" being quite convinced the object was real. The hall being dark, and the time just dusk in the evening, she did not feel fear until the object vanished on her approaching it.

Well, it appeared several times afterwards, indeed so commonly that they got used to it, and on the man coming home he was told in a chaffing manner to look out for the ghost. Of course he did not believe it, but one evening about 9 o'clock he got up from his chair and went upstairs, when halfway up he saw a woman standing, and so close was she that he was right through her before he could stop himself. That same night he awoke from his sleep, and felt there was someone in the room. He was lying with his face to the wall, and the gas burning low behind him, so he turned round, and there was a Nurse standing by his bedside. Without thinking he said, "What the devil do you want here?" and sat up in bed, and the apparition faded away. He saw it several times afterwards, and so did the others, but it was a tame ghost and did no harm.

Now I cannot explain or account for the remarkable happenings in my own house, but the stories I have told are true, and I know that the people who took the house after us only stayed three months and then left on account of the unaccountable noises and manifestations experienced, so I will leave my readers to draw their own conclusions, and with that conclude this chapter, which was written while crossing the Arabian sea, in the year of our Lord 1907, on board the good steamer Telemachus bound from Jeddah to Penang and beyond with 930 Pilgrims. Hence the account in the early part of this chapter of my first experience of Pilgrim carrying. I don't think it so interesting as I did then, nor would my reader either, if they were living over the combined smell of dried Fish, Garlic, Coconut Oil, and human beings who had not washed their clothes for months, and carbolic acid, a most lovely and sweet-smelling savour.

# Chapter 9

*1894 Master of the Ajax—difficult lading at Ymuiden—
joins the Polyphemus—drinking in New York—
women afloat—Robert Nelson dies*

About the 5th February 1894, I received word from the Office that they would require a Master for the S.S. Ajax, sailing from Liverpool for China about the 23rd February, and, if I was well enough, they would like me to go in her, but that I must first go away for a week to make sure I could stand a change. After consulting with the Doctor, my wife and I went to Llandudno for a week. So beneficial was the change that I did not have an attack whilst there, but improved very much.

I joined the S.S. Ajax on the 20th February, and as she was a type of steamer now no more, I will just say a few words about her. She was one of the three original ships that the Company started with in the year 1866, they being the first steamers which steamed round the Cape of Good Hope to the Far East, and made a financial success of it.

The names of the three were Agamemnon, Ajax, and Achilles. They were beautiful models, built of the best Iron, with a deep keel and barque rigged, and would manoeuvre under sail. They had compound tandem engines, that is, the high pressure on top of the low pressure Cylinder, with a big flywheel to regulate the revolutions of the propeller. They also had their propellers abaft the rudder, the latter occupying the space where the propeller is in ordinary steamers. The rudder was in two halves, connected by two oval rings, through which the shaft ran to the bush in the stern post. I found the Ajax a splendid sea boat, but owing to the want of rudder power, a most difficult ship to manoeuvre in narrow waters. The top of her rudder only reached the 18 ft. 6 in. mark, and as she drew 24 ft. 6 in. when loaded, a seaman reader will understand why she was bad to manoeuvre. The only way to avoid a danger was to give her full speed and go for it. Many a time my hair felt like standing on end, but we used to pull through somehow. I may mention that I joined her on her 56th voyage to China, and her yards had been done away with and she was then rigged as a three-masted schooner.

We left Liverpool on the 23rd February 1894, but as the weather was very dirty I put into Moelfra Bay [Anglesey] and lay there all night. We got away next day, and arrived at Algiers on the 4th March, thence on to Penang, Singapore, Hong Kong, Amoy, and Shanghai. On the voyage home we had Pilgrims for Jeddah, and on the 2nd day of June, while in Lat. 8° N. and 56° E., our connecting rod broke and we drifted round in a strong Monsoon and high sea for four days, and having then effected temporary repairs, we crawled into Perim on the 11th June, remaining there for five days for further repairs, which were only temporary after all. However, they took us to Amsterdam and London alright, but on the passage round to Liverpool we broke down again. I managed however to get into Falmouth Roads, and after 24 hours delay there, we proceeded to Liverpool. My Chief Engineer always suffered badly from Java Fever when there was an accident, but I at last found out it was 'Whisky Fever' he suffered from, and then his name was 'Walker'.

On the 5th August we sailed again for Algiers, China and Japan, but there was not much worthy of note on this voyage, things going smoothly throughout. We carried a few passengers during the voyage, calling at Foochow for Tea, and Jeddah with Pilgrims and Cargo. We also called at Nagasaki on the voyage, and I there made the acquaintance of Captain F. Devenish, who had just been appointed Company's Pilot for the Inland Sea of Japan. We struck up a warm friendship there, which has continued ever since.

We arrived at London on the 2nd December, and word came that the ship would be laid up for quite three months, but on the 5th January 1895, the Company found that she was wanted for the berth, so they had to hurry up and get her ready. Sailing from London on the 9th January, we arrived at Liverpool on the 12th January. I may mention that on the passage home I received a circular from Messrs. Alfred Holt & Co, saying that owing to bad times, they felt compelled to reduce the wages of the Masters and Officers. The reduction was 15% off our standing pay, and 50% off all bonuses and Pilgrim money. This meant £100 a year in my case, but we had to accept it or leave it. However, at the close of the year the Company thanked us all for our loyal support and gave us a Special Bonus of £30, they having done much better than was expected. But it was not until the year 1898 that matters were put on their old footing, indeed a better one as far as I was concerned.

We sailed from Liverpool on the 23rd January 1895, and had bad weather leaving, indeed so bad that I could not land my Liverpool Pilot, but carried him on to Algiers, for which port we had cargo. We then proceeded on our voyage to Yokohama, via ports. This was an uneventful voyage, and we arrived at Amsterdam on the 19th June, and then proceeded to London. After some little time there, the owners decided to send her to Amsterdam, dry-dock her, and transfer her to the Dutch Flag, and put her in the Java trade.

I was sent to take her there, superintend matters, and then bring her to Liverpool. Now, although it was summer time, there was very bad weather in the North Sea. The ship was very light, and for some unexplained reason, rather short of Coal. I only joined her the day of sailing, taking my wife and daughter Bessie with me. When we arrived off Ymuiden [Netherlands] at about 8 a.m., it was blowing a heavy S.W. gale, so I would not risk going in, and stood her off to the Westward. The engineer then came up and told me there was only half a day's coal on board. Now, I had taken the ship over from the London Overlooker as fit and ready for sea. He never mentioned coals, neither did I, taking it for granted all was in order. This was my mistake, and one which nearly ended in disaster. We waited all day in hopes that the gale would moderate but at 4 p.m. decided that I would run into Harbour, the wind having hauled more Westerly, the weather clearing and the tide slack.

Ymuiden is a very bad place to run for in a S.Westerly gale, but I was on a lee shore, and short of coals, so it was 'Hobson's Choice'—do or die. When we got within half a mile from the Breakwaters, there was a big ground sea running, and the ship was being thrown about like a toy boat, and as we entered between the Breakwaters, a big S.W'ly sea took and lifted her up and threw her broadside on, straight at the North Breakwater. Why she did not strike it, I don't know, but I think the back-wash threw her off, for she rolled over on her starboard beam ends, recovered herself, and rushed into the Harbour, and was practically safe, though we did some damage inside before I could stop her, having gone in full speed as the only way to save the ship. My wife got a terrible fright, and I don't think she has ever been quite happy on board a ship since, and, as a matter of fact, we always seem to have narrow escapes when she is on board, and she is a perfect 'Jonah' for fogs.

Before I conclude my account of the Ajax, I will tell a little story about her, which is too good to be lost. On one of her voyages to Shanghai while under the Command of her first Master—Captain Kidd—she was lying in Shanghai River, when something went wrong with her shaft, which necessitated the tail-end being uncoupled from the other parts. After this was done, work was suspended for the night. There was no thought of danger, and no lashings were put on the tail end but, during the night, the tide caught the propeller and it began to revolve, gradually working out the shaft, until the flange caught the bush, which it smashed, and the water began to run into the ship. All on board were now asleep, excepting a Quartermaster on watch. He noticed that the lower part of the gangway ladder was in the water, so he pulled it up, repeating this two or three times. The ship meanwhile was slowly sinking, and no-one the wiser, until the water began to run through the cabin ports into the stewards' bunks. This of course roused everyone out, and they lowered the boats and got into them. On the enquiry as to the cause of the accident, the Quartermaster told his tale of the gangway ladder, and in reply to questions said that he thought the tide was rising, and thus kept covering the ladder. Oh! Shades of Nelson! What an answer. I regret to say that Captain Kidd was washed overboard from the Ajax in the Bay of Biscay during a heavy N.W. gale in September 1883. The Ajax was sold to the Italians about 1898, and was broken up for scrap iron. She is now probably part of an Italian Battleship.

On the 4th September 1895, I joined the S.S. Polyphemus in London, and took her round to Glasgow and Liverpool. She was a very fine ship of 1,800 tons register, and carried about 20 Cabin passengers. She had a speed of 12 knots and was four years old when I joined her. She also had steam steering-gear, the first I had been with, and I felt very proud of being given Command of her. We sailed from Liverpool on the 5th October, with passengers and cargo, for Algiers, China and Japan, calling at Colombo for Coal. On our arrival at Yokohama, it was decided to load the ship homewards on the New York berth, via usual Chinese ports, but we were detained in Shanghai for three weeks, owing to the Northern Rivers being frozen up, and no cargo boats able to get down.

However, we left Shanghai on the 9th January 1896, and finished loading at Penang, at which port I went half shares with our Agent in two Leopards and I also had two Japanese Poodle Dogs. These I sold in New York at a good profit.

We called at Algiers for coal and provisions, leaving there on February 18th 1896 for New York. We had boisterous weather on the way over, and it took us 20 days to make the passage. On 12th March we experienced a blizzard in New York, which blocked the whole place up with snow and ice.

While in New York I had an amusing experience with the American Customs Officers. It appears that animals of all kinds are liable to duty and should be entered on the manifest. I—not knowing this—did not report them to the boarding officer, but did so at the Custom House. On the day after the blizzard I had a visit from two Secret Service Officers, who had power to seize the animals, and subject me to a fine, not exceeding $500. After some talk on deck, I said, "Gentlemen, it is too cold to talk here, come down to my cabin." Now the cabin was nice and cosy, and I made them comfortable, and then said to them before proceeding to business, "Gentlemen, what will you take to drink? I have some real good French Brandy, such as one rarely sees. Now which shall it be, that or some real old Scotch Whisky?"

"Well," they said, "I guess Captain, we will try the Brandy."

So the steward brought the Brandy and a full box of Cigars. After sampling the Brandy &c., one of the officers said, "Captain, there are no flies on either of these two articles. Now I have a friend up the wharf and he would be tickled to death if he could just taste this Brandy."

Well, his friend came with another friend, and between them they finished the bottle of Brandy and another half one besides. They also emptied the box of Cigars into their pockets, and then rose to go, so I said, "Gentlemen, I have been much pleased to have your company this afternoon, but what am I to do about the Leopards and Dogs?"

They replied, "Captain, you have treated us like white men, and we never go back on a man who does that. Damn the Leopards!" Of course that was good enough for me, but the fun of it was, both the Brandy and Cigars should have paid duty.

After I had been in New York a few days, I took leave, and went down to Norfolk, Virginia, for the purpose of seeing my wife's Uncle and Aunt Stephen, also cousins. After seeing them, I went to Baltimore, Washington, and Annapolis. At the latter place my Uncle Robert Goodwin's daughter Bessie lived. She was married to a Mr Girault, and had a family of four daughters and three sons. I found them all very nice and quite enjoyed my short visit. On my return to New York, my cousin, William Bryson came from Chicago to see me, and I was exceedingly pleased to see him again. We spent three pleasant days together. I may mention that my wife's Uncle—Captain Stephen—was the Pilot of the Confederate Ironclad Merrimac when she fought the Federal Monitor, the first fight between Ironclads the world had ever seen [1862]. Strange to say, about two years after meeting Uncle, I met a man who was one of the Quartermasters on the Monitor during the fight, so I got a good account of the engagement from both sides.

At New York we loaded partly for China and partly for Liverpool, sailing for the latter port on March 25th 1896, and arriving there April 8th, having had a fine passage across. While on this voyage, and on December 5th 1895, my son—John Henry, who was then sixteen years of age—went to serve his apprenticeship, as a Marine Engineer, with Messrs. D. Rollo & Sons, Liverpool. This was his own choice, and if his desire as a lad to see the inside of every machine he came across, and take all the clocks in the house to pieces, forgetting to put them together again, was any criterion of his aptitude for the profession, his mother was right in thinking he had a bright future before him. I confess I would sooner he had followed my profession, but in that way of thinking I don't follow my father, who told me he would sooner apprentice me to a chimney-sweep than to the sea, saying it was a dog's life. My mother hoped I would be a Schoolmaster. Why, I don't know, for I had as much aptitude for it as a Bull has for handling a musket. But all parents have dreams for their children, though very few have them realized.

Returning to my son, I may say he has so far done even better than I expected, having passed his Chief Engineer's examination with credit. But then there was a girl on the end of the string, which accounts for a good deal in this life, and candidly I don't think he would have worried if he had been fancy-free.

I was only home nine days and then started out for the usual China and Japan voyage, sailing on the 18th April. On this voyage I had my daughter Meg with me, she having been ill some two years, suffering from Anaemia, and our Doctor having recommended a complete change, this was an ideal way of giving her one, as my ship carried a Doctor and stewardess. I may say now, that the voyage did her much good, and that she was very lucky in going on this particular trip, for she saw more of the world than she would have done on other voyages, for, in addition to the usual ports, we called at Algiers, Colombo, Foochow, Amoy, Coconado, Madras, Cuddalore, and Marseilles, and had a lot of passengers most of the time. I consider she was a lucky girl, particularly as we stopped carrying passengers shortly afterwards, and all womenfolk—well nearly all— were forbidden to sail in the ships, that is, on Oversea voyages, but the Captain, mate, and Chief Engineer, may take their wives round the Coast.

In theory I am opposed to females sailing in the same ship with their husbands or fathers, but theory is all very well when you don't apply it to yourself. At the same time I have often in time of stress and danger felt comforted with the thought that my wife was safe at home. Still I should dearly like to take her and my daughter Bessie with me on one voyage just to let them see the World as I have seen it, but I fear my wish will never be realized, and I will have to go on pulling my lonely oar all by my own little self, as my daughter Bess used to say when she was a three-year-old.

In due course we arrived at Marseilles and after two or three days there, proceeded on our voyage to London, but in the Bay of Biscay we experienced a heavy N.W. gale and as we were light and all the cargo in the bottom of the ship, she rolled fearfully, indeed I never saw a ship roll like it before or since. Our lady passengers were very much frightened, and at about 10 p.m. the steward got to me on the bridge, and said he could not pacify them, and would I come and assure them there was no danger. When I got into the Saloon, I found the water washing about, and the ladies in it, some holding on to the legs of the table, others letting themselves wash about, and all in despair. Comforting them with the assurance that we were in no immediate danger, and that in two more hours we would be clear of Ushant, and then keep before the sea, and thus minimise the rolling, they were persuaded to get into their beds. One lady I picked out of the water and lifted her on to the cabin settee, blocking her off from the table with cushions, but while attending to another lady the ship gave a tremendous roll and lurch, lifted the lady off the settee, threw her over the table, and dropped her on the outside settee, from which she slid over to the other side of the Saloon, mixed in an indescribable heap with myself, the other lady, and stewards. After this episode there was no comforting these two ladies, so I told the steward to lash them to a stanchion, and got back on deck, for the rolling made me very anxious. However we came through all right, and arrived in London on September 24th 1896, but I never again want to see a vessel roll like the Polyphemus did that night.

While in Marseilles my wife wrote me that my old friend and shipmate—Captain R. Nelson—had passed away suddenly. His death was a great blow to his family, friends, and shipmates, for a finer seaman, a more kindly-hearted genial man never trod a ship's deck. He and I came through some hard times and weathered some tight corners together, and I always found him staunch and true, ever resourceful and ready with a helping hand. A fit epitaph for him would be "Faithful below he did his duty, and now he has gone aloft."

There is a little story of my old friend which just occurred to my mind. When the French were having a small dispute with the Chinese Government, which led to the French Fleet operating on the Coast of China and Formosa [Taiwan], Robert was in Command of the S.S. Myrmidon and was on one occasion stopped in the Formosa Channel by a French cruiser and searched for contraband of War. Now in addition to the French Officer being very offensive in his manner, Bob had all an Englishman's antagonism to being interfered with on the High Seas, and his temper had risen to boiling point. As the French Lieutenant was about to go down the Gangway ladder, he turned to Robert and said, "What is your name, Sir?"

The latter promptly answered, "My name, Sir, is Nelson, one which is well known to your countrymen," the result of this answer being 'Sacres', 'Blue Lights', and 'Rockets' on the Frenchman's part.

While I write, many episodes of our younger days crowd through my mind like a tumbling sea. How plainly I can see the old Comorin rushing to destruction on the Skerries in a S.W. gale, steering gear gone, towing hawser ported, and dragging astern, all hands, as usual, drunk leaving Liverpool, and not recovered when the stress came, Bob, myself, and two younger lads being the only available hands to get sail on the ship. Bob and I loosed the fore topsail, which was fortunately double-reefed. We got it sheeted home, after a fashion, with the aid of the hand winch, and got the fore topmast staysail on her and just managed to pay her off the danger in time. Dark night though it was, we could see the sea breaking over the rocks, and when all was over, Bob took me by the hand and said, "John, my lad, we will never be nearer death than we were to-night without getting there." But before we parted company he and I were fated to come near to death's door on more than one occasion, but, by God's mercy, were brought safely through every danger.

I will now close this chapter, but before doing so, I may mention that our Purser—Mr Rorison—who is kindly copying out this chapter of my manuscript, is the son of an old fellow-apprentice of mine, and the grandson of Captain Rorison, who was Master of the Calcutta trader Thomas Brocklebank, 550 tons register, when my father was Chief Officer of her.

Thus are the toilers of the sea linked together from generation to generation.

# Chapter 10

I left Liverpool in the Polyphemus on the 9th October 1896, bound for China and Japan, after a 15 days stay at home. This included the passage round from London to Liverpool. Our voyage out was uneventful but on arrival at Yokohama we were fixed to load homewards on the New York berth. In due course we arrived at Shanghai, staying there 14 days, during which time we had three cases of Smallpox amongst the crew, two of which proved fatal.

From Shanghai we went to Amoy for 1,000 tons of Tea, and then proceeded to Hong Kong and Singapore, taking from the latter port 100 Pilgrims for Jeddah, and some cargo for New York, at which port we arrived on the 13th March 1897, after a fine passage of 15½ days from Algiers.

While the ship was in New York I went down to Annapolis to see my cousin, Bessie Girault, and my wife's Uncle Stephen pressed me to come and see them, but for various reasons and want of time, I could not go. I have often very much regretted this, as Uncle was a fine sample of an old seaman, and as I have not been to New York since, and he has gone to his long home, I am left regretting that I did not go.

My cousin, William Bryson, again came from Chicago to see me, and spent two or three days in New York. I have not seen him since, but he and his wife were over on a European Tour in 1904, and called to see my wife and family, as they returned home through Liverpool. I am given to understand from other cousins in America that William is a very rich man. He has not told me so himself, but my wife tells me he is the same genial unassuming man that he was when she and I saw him first in 1864, and that riches do not seem to have spoiled him.

We loaded a full cargo in New York for Glasgow, and arrived at the latter port on the 16th of April 1897 after a passage of 12 days 18 hours.

We again loaded on the China and Japan berth at Liverpool, sailing thence on the 7th May. This voyage being the last one on which we carried Cabin passengers—the Company for various reasons giving up that part of their trade—we had as many as we could accommodate, amongst them, Mr G. Holt, the eldest son of our principal Owner. There is nothing to record of the outward passage, indeed all went well with us to Singapore, at which port I hoped to load homeward, but business was very bad owing to over-competition, so we were ordered to proceed to Coconada, on the East Coast of India, to load a full cargo for Marseilles at a very low rate of freight.

We left Coconada on 22nd August, and called at Colombo for Coal, sailing thence on the 26th August. On the evening of the 7th September—the ship being then 27 miles North of Jebel Tier, in the Red Sea—we found our crank shaft was nearly broken in two, so I paddled her down to the Westward into 36 fathoms of water, and anchored. We then proceeded to change the crank shaft, having a spare one on board. This took us five days, the weather in the meantime being fearfully hot, indeed, with one exception, the hottest I have ever experienced.

While lying at anchor, a French mail steamer came close by us and asked if we wanted assistance. This I declined, but requested her to report me with crank shaft broken, but repairing. He promised to do so at Jibbute, but forgot. However, after passing Perim, he remembered, and seeing a homeward bound English steamer, signalled her. What he told her has never been clearly made out. Suffice it to say the Englishman went into Perim and reported the Polyphemus lost on Jebel Tier with 28 hands. This was at once wired home, and that evening—Saturday—the papers came out with big headlines, 'Loss Of A Liverpool Liner'.

By a lucky chance when the evening paper was brought to my house, the girls got hold of it first, and promptly hid it, so that their Mother should not see the bad news. Now the little mother happened to be very anxious to see if there was any news of me in the paper, and she kept asking if the paper had come, and the girls had no alternative but to say, "No!" their idea being to keep the news from their Mother in the hope that there would be a better account on Monday. However, the Office people, while hoping for the best, thought it their duty to write to our brother-in-law—W. Parry— asking him to tell my wife that they did not credit the news, but it was as well to be prepared for the worst, so, whilst the girls were at Church—they had all gone there to keep out of their Mother's way—W. Parry's eldest daughter came round to tell her Aunt the bad news.

So that Saturday an expedition started out from Perim to look for us, and on the Sunday at 5 a.m. we finished the job and proceeded on our voyage. At 8 a.m. I spoke to the Company's steamer Sarpedon in the usual way. She passed Perim on the Monday morning and was called into port by signal and ordered to turn back and look for me. The Captain was amused and said, "Why, I saw her yesterday morning on the usual track, and got her 'All Well' signals." This was at once wired home, and on Monday evening my wife had thirteen telegrams telling her the good news. She told me she had no idea she had so many friends, but all the same it was very good of those who wired her.

We arrived at Marseilles in due course, and after discharging our cargo, proceeded to Liverpool in ballast. This was owing to a mistake of the Owners, as we had a full cargo engaged for London. If I had made the mistake, I should, figuratively, have been hung in chains like a Pirate. However, we arrived at Liverpool on the 5th October 1897, and I found myself quite a hero, all because I did not lose my ship. Anyhow, I never, before or since, had such a warm welcome from my Owners.

After about a month home, I again left Liverpool on the usual Eastern voyage, sailing on the 11th November and arriving at Port Said on the 25th, after rather a rough passage. We steamed on to Singapore direct from Suez, and thence on to Hong Kong, arriving there on

Christmas Day 1897. After calling at the usual ports in Japan, and China, we arrived back at Singapore on the 20th February 1898, loading homeward on the London and Amsterdam berth. We also had as passengers from Singapore to Jeddah, the Sultan of Sulu and about a dozen of his wives, also his Prime Minister and Treasurer. The Sultana—his principal wife—was a very nice pleasant woman and could talk a little English. As she was by no means her husband's favourite, she was allowed more liberty than the others. I often had a talk with her, but always in the presence of the Prime Minister, who appeared to be the watch-dog.

I met Captain Nish at Singapore, not having seen him for a good while. He and I are the best of friends, and I am always pleased to see him. Here follows a good story which is characteristic of him. The old gentleman is a gruff, but warm-hearted sailor. He has many superstitions, one of them being that it is very unlucky to play cards on Sunday on shipboard. (Please note I am not defending the practice either ashore or afloat.) Well, a voyage or two previous to our meeting, he had two Missionaries—passengers from China to London— and one Sunday afternoon the steward came and told him they were playing cards in the Saloon.

"Are they," he said, "by God, I'll soon stop that."

Walking into the Saloon he swept up the cards from the table and turning to the Missionaries, he said, "Do you want to sink the bl---y ship?" walked out and threw the cards overboard, leaving the Missionaries in such a state of amazement that they could not say a word in reply.

Returning to my narrative, I may add that we left

Singapore on the 26th February, bound for Penang and Colombo, and at 3 a.m. on the 5th March our shaft broke in about the middle of its length. After four day's work, we got it connected with clips, and proceeded dead slow to Colombo, arriving there five days late and finding one of our ships on the point of starting out to look for us. During the time we were drifting the Sultan was greatly alarmed, and sent for me, several times, to ask what I would do for his safety if it came on to blow or we got short of provisions. I told him that in any case he and his favourite lady would be well cared for, and that he need not he alarmed. This satisfied him for a few hours, when he would again send and ask the same question. However, we transferred him to the other ship at Colombo, and so got clear of his doubts, fears and Harem.

We remained in Colombo 21 days repairing, during which time I went up to Kandy—the Capital of Ceylon—and there saw some of the relics of Buddha and other interesting sights. Kandy is an exceedingly pretty place, and I have never seen a City I was as much taken up with, or derived more pleasure from seeing.

We left Colombo on the 31st March 1898, and arrived at Amsterdam on the 29th April. There I received a letter from my Owners, telling me that they were going to put the Polyphemus under the Dutch Flag, and into the Java Trade, and that they would rather I did not go into that trade on account of my having had the Fever so badly. They also told me they were building new ships, and that I should have the second one launched if I chose to wait ashore about three months, but leaving the matter for me to decide. Although I was not at all alarmed at the prospect of going into the Java trade, my wife was, so I decided to stay back, the Manager— Mr Crompton—promising me that I should be employed taking the ships round the Coast. I had plenty of work to do, but very little pay for doing it, and instead of three months at home, it was seven, owing to strikes amongst the men at the Building Yard, which delayed the ships. In fact, at the end of the seventh month, my Owners sent for and told me the ships would be four months before they were ready, but that the S.S. Dardanus required a Master for her coming voyage, and if it suited, I could take her and be back in time for the new ship. As the past seven months had been a financial failure, I decided to go.

The Dardanus was a vessel of 2,900 tons register, and was then a modern cargo boat, having triple expansion engines and a speed of 11 knots on a consumption of 34 tons Welsh coal per day. The accommodation for Master and Officers was very poor, and placed amidships. Although glad to get her at the time, I never liked the ship. However, I took her to Barrow-in-Furness, and loaded 1,800 tons of Railway Iron for Singapore, returning to Liverpool to finish loading for the usual Japanese Ports. We sailed on the 10th December 1898, and arrived in London on the 20th April 1899, only to find all the new ships afloat and masters appointed to them.

This was a great disappointment to me, and I don't think to this day I was treated fairly in the matter from beginning to end, but the Manager was a man who, whenever he had done you a favour, always considered you owed the Company something, and took it out of you later on, for in both cases where I had experience of this little trait of his, it cost me a good round sum of money, and much bitterness of spirit.

On my going down to Liverpool, the Owners informed me that they wished me to go in the S.S. Diomed, 3,005 tons register, a ship of the same type as the Dardanus, but with many improvements on the latter. This ship I liked very much, and left her with regret after being in her for nearly three eventful years.

We sailed from Liverpool on the 6th May 1899, after about two weeks stay home, and proceeded on the usual China and Japan voyage, calling at Jeddah for about 500 Pilgrims, amongst whom the Smallpox broke out, and we had about 14 deaths.

On arrival we were of course quarantined, and after five days detention—no fresh cases having occurred— orders came off that we were to vaccinate the whole crowd. It took all day to complete the operation, and we were very glad when the task was finished.

There is not much to record of this voyage, except that we called at Foochow, on the way home, for Tea, and that up to the present time (1907) I have not again visited that port. Its only trade was Tea, and that has almost gone, owing to the competition of Indian and Ceylon Teas. After Foochow, we called at Singapore, Penang, Colombo, and Gibraltar, arriving in London on the 23rd September, and on the 29th we sailed for Swansea, my wife joining me there. After about a week's stay there, we sailed for Liverpool, and as usual when my wife is on board, had dense fogs on the passage round, and had more than one narrow escape of being run down, or running some other ship down.

On arrival at Liverpool, I found that arrangements had been made for us to take out Naval reliefs to Hong Kong, the draft consisting of three officers, and 400 sailors and marines, sailing on the 20th October 1899.

While I was at home the Boers declared War against us, and on the eve of sailing news reached us of the victory of Elandslaagte, which, alas, was the last victory for us for some time, as many weary months of anxiety and disaster followed.

It is none of my business to write a history of the war, but I cannot help saying we brought it on ourselves, by our cocksureness and despising of the Boers. Only a few thinking men would believe the War had to come, and the leader of these was that great Statesman, Joseph Chamberlain. I, personally, was a humble follower of his, having followed the course of events in South Africa since the Majuba disaster [British defeat by Boers, 1881], for which I shall always hold Mr Gladstone's vacillating policy responsible. In my opinion the British Nation is made up of a few wise men, and the balance irresponsible babblers and fools, always poking their fingers into other people's pie when the latter are in power, and then, when the owner of the pie protests, and tells them to come on if they dare, it is, "Oh, we don't want to fight, we were only shaking our moral finger at you, besides, we are not ready to fight, we have reduced our Army, and what soldiers we have are armed with obsolete weapons, but you really must be good, or we shall have to buy some new guns and come and beat you."

And so it has gone on all my life, except when we had a strong man like Disraeli in power, and I am quite sure if Joseph Chamberlain had been listened to when he wanted the Government to prepare months before they did, the War would never have occurred, for the Boers would not have dared to declare it. But the Government (Unionist) were playing to the Peace Party, the same party which has cost the Country millions of money by preaching and practising, when they could, false economy. They hate the Army, and have always done their best to cripple it. They don't like the Navy any more than they do the Army. Public opinion however is a little too strong for them, but they do their best to starve it.

Two or three times in my life, and always under a Liberal Government, we had to eat 'Humble Pie' because we had no Fleet to send to sea, (Mr Gladstone again). In fact the 'Liberal peace at any price faction' are like the five foolish virgins whose lamps were not trimmed. Never ready, and don't want to be is their motto, until someone by chance, treads on their favourite corn. They then insist on the Whole Army being sent to smash the offender, and denounce the Government because they cannot comply with their demands. Now I strongly deprecate bullying in any shape, but I do say we ought to be in a position to prevent others from bullying us. Anti-Militarists can say what they like, but the man behind the gun has the last word.

To return to my story. After sailing from Liverpool with the troops all went well with us, but we called into Malta for Coal. This was the first, and up to the present, the only time I have visited the Island, which is a nest of begging monks and nuns.

We had a very pleasant trip out to Hong Kong, and everyone was satisfied with the result of our carrying the troops. We came home on the usual route, calling at Amoy for Chinese passengers for Singapore, and at Jeddah with cargo and Pilgrims, arriving at London on the 22nd February. We left there on 6th March for Cardiff, to load 2,000 tons rails for a place called Kagoshima, in Japan, which at this time was closed to foreign trade, but as the rails were for the Japanese Government, we received a permit to go there to discharge. This was the most interesting trip to Japan I ever made, Kagoshima being a purely Japanese town, beautifully kept, and no Europeans living in or near it. It is the birthplace of their great national hero 'Saigo' and they have an immense bronze statue of him, which is almost worshipped by the residents. The first thing a Japanese asks you when be hears you have been to Kagoshima, is, "Did you see Saigo?"—just in the same way as the Sydney folk ask a new arrival, "How do you like our Harbour?" Anyhow it is a fine statue, and next to Kandy, I liked Kagoshima better than any Eastern town I have visited.

I may mention that we called at Algiers, outwards, to load a quantity of Flour for Jeddah, and then on to Perim to load a lot of old telegraph wire for Shanghai, finishing our outward passage at Yokohama. We loaded homewards, commencing at Hong Kong and going on to Singapore and Colombo, thence on to Liverpool, arriving there 2nd August 1900, thus finishing one more epoch of a life of wandering to and fro over the face of the waters.

# Chapter 11

During my absence on the last voyage, the Company I served had quietly established a Line to Australia from Glasgow, outwards round the Cape of Good Hope to Adelaide, Melbourne, Sydney, and Brisbane, and homewards through the Suez Canal in the Wool season, and round the Cape in the off season.

I had long desired to go to Australia, perhaps because both myself and wife had many relations there, or because I never had an opportunity of going, therefore desired it the more. However, I was delighted when our Owner informed me that the S.S. Diomed was to proceed to Barry and load a full cargo of Coal for Hong Kong, after due discharge of which she was to proceed to a place called Port Pirie, in Spencer's Gulf, and there take in 1,000 tons of Ore, thence on to Sydney and Melbourne to fill up with Wool. Apart from my wish to visit Australia, this particular route was one I had a strong desire to go over in a steamer. Of course a great portion was familiar to me, both by sail and steam, but I wanted to do it consecutively, so it can be quite understood that I was pleased. The old adage which says 'All things come to him who waits' had at least come true in my case.

On the 18th August 1900 we sailed from Liverpool to Barry to load 5,000 tons of Coal, arriving there the next day, only to find the coal miners on strike, and all work stopped. I may mention that my wife and daughter Bessie came with me, and we had quite a long time in Barry, nearly three weeks. Unfortunately, my wife took very ill, but recovered before I left, so that this anxiety was removed from my mind before sailing. I will now give the names of the officers of the Diomed for I may have occasion to mention them later on. Mr Hughes was Chief Officer with me all the time I was in her, and Mr Bebb, who had been third officer, was this voyage promoted to second, and a Mr Wallace joined as third, Mr Cable being Chief Engineer.

On the 7th September, I sent my wife and Bessie home by train and this next day I sailed, having previously received instructions to run at a speed of ten knots until arrival at Port Pirie. We coaled at Port Said, and Singapore, and on the passage up to Hong Kong encountered a typhoon, for which we hove to until the centre had passed to the Westward of us, finally arriving at Hong Kong on 21st October.

We sailed from there in water ballast on 4th November, taking the route down through Stoltz Channel, Gaspar Straits, and Sunda Straits, passing close to Christmas Island, now celebrated for its Phosphate deposits, and thence on to Cape Lewin, the western and stormy cape of Australia, arriving at Port Pirie on 24th November, after a passage of 20 days 9 hours.

I found Port Pirie a dull, uninteresting place, its only business being the shipment and smelting of Ore from the Broken Hill Mines. We managed to put in eleven days there, and then sailed for Sydney, arriving on 9th December 1900.

Sydney is a very fine English town, and I can only describe the Harbour as beautiful. One is often asked, "Which is the finest Harbour, Sydney, Rio de Janeiro, or San Francisco?" They are all fine Harbours, but I class them as follows: Rio, grand and imposing, 'Frisco, big, fretful, and dreary, and Sydney, fine, lovely, and joyous.

I had not been long in Sydney before my sister—Mrs Annie Maxwell—was on board. She and her family had a firm at a place called Liverpool, about 20 miles outside of Sydney, and, as soon as possible, I went out to see her and the children. She had three, viz. Ellie, Flossie, and Ernest. Her husband—Alfred Maxwell—had gone to the Boer War in the New South Wales Mounted Rifles. He was wounded at Diamond Hill, also got kicked by a horse, and contracted Typhoid Fever. While I was in Australia, he was invalided home, and granted a passage to England, returning to the Antipodes before I reached home.

I spent a most enjoyable time in Sydney, leaving there on Christmas morning 1900, my sister Annie accompanying me to Melbourne. On arrival there, my cousins, John M. Goodwin and Ella Robinson, met me. The latter had lived in England with us in her young days, going to Australia in 1862. The former was born in Australia, being the son of my Father's younger brother Joseph. John is a very fine fellow, and I became quite attached to him, and looked forward to seeing him each voyage I made to Australia. I also met his brother,

Samuel, who was at that time running a big Dairy Farm near Melbourne. Sam is a typical Australian Bushman, having been for some years Manager of a big Cattle run up-country. My wife's relations also looked me up. Her Aunt, Mrs Rae and family, which consisted of two married daughters, two single ones, and a son James, who when a boy paid a visit to England and saw his home relations. They were exceedingly kind to me.

We remained a week in Melbourne, which I found very short for all the visiting I had to do. My sister Annie stayed in Melbourne with Ella Robinson for a week after I left, which I did on the 3rd January 1901, bound for Dunkirk, London, and Antwerp. We made a splendid passage to Suez, steaming there in 28 days, 22 hours, without a stop for any purpose.

On the evening of the 26th January, an English steamer, just out from Aden, signalled us the death of our beloved Queen Victoria. This was sad and unexpected news for us, and cast quite a gloom over the ship for days.

We arrived at Dunkirk on the 14th February, sailing again on the 17th for London, and leaving the latter port for Antwerp on the 20th. Had this been a summer instead of a winter voyage, my wife would have joined me in Dunkirk, but, she being such a bad sailor, I would rather forego the pleasure of her company than subject her to the discomfort of travelling and seasickness. She would have been only too willing to come at any sacrifice to herself, but I could not permit it. We remained in Antwerp for about six days and then sailed to Cardiff for the purpose of dry-docking and bunkering. After rounding Land's End, we got a very heavy S.W. gale, and the ship being in water-ballast, we had quite a rough time with her, but I managed to get behind Lundy Island, staying there for the night, which was a very wild one, and I was thankful my dear little wife was safe at home. On my arrival at Cardiff, I received instructions to hand over the ship to Mr Hughes, who would take her to Glasgow, I going to Liverpool for holiday. Of course this pleased both myself and Mr Hughes, who however got such a dressing down on the passage that he came to the conclusion it was not all 'pie' being in Command.

At Glasgow the ship loaded a general cargo for Australia, and I joined her on the 28th March 1901. On the evening of the 29th, we had a heavy snow-storm, our decks being a foot deep in snow next morning. The weather looked threatening, and the barometer was down to 28.30, the lowest I had seen in Great Britain for a very long time. However, we left the dock and made the best of our way to Greenock. On arrival there my brother, who was Overlooker in Glasgow and had accompanied me down the River, suggested that I should anchor until the weather improved, but while discussing the matter, I saw a break in the clouds to the N.W. and looking at the barometer saw it had begun to rise. As a general rule, the first rise after low indicates a stronger blow, but I had formed an opinion that in this case the worst had passed with the snowstorm. Further, I always disliked anchoring in a home port when outward bound, preferring to get away and have done with it, so I said to my brother, "I think the weather is going to fine up in a moderate way, and that the barometer will rise rapidly, and taking everything into consideration, I have decided to go on."

He did not agree with me, and said, "A wilful man will have his own way," so bidding him Good-bye, I put her full speed ahead, and started on my long journey of 12,100 miles round the Cape to Port Adelaide. My estimate of the weather proved correct. It cleared up beautifully, and we had but little wind, with a rapidly rising glass.

We made the passage out to Adelaide in 44 days 6 hours, but deducting difference in time, we were really only 43 days 20 hours. This was considered a splendid steaming feat, as our engines never stopped for any purpose from the day we left until we arrived at Adelaide, for which great credit was due to the Chief Engineer and staff.

We were two days in Adelaide, two in Melbourne and three in Sydney, and then went on to Brisbane, arriving there on the 25th May. I found the latter port a very pretty place, and was much taken with it. I forgot to mention that my cousin, John Goodwin, and my wife's cousin's (Mary Burniston) son Leslie, came on the run from Melbourne to Brisbane and back with me, enjoying their trip very much. The Captain could take a friend under the old management, but under the present regime that privilege had been stopped.

We arrived in Sydney on the 30th May, and I of course saw my sister, husband, and family. Alfred looked very well, but suffered occasionally from Fever and Ague, which he contracted in South Africa. We remained in Sydney for eight days and then left, on to Melbourne, berthing the ship at Williamstown and remaining there for five days, during which time I saw as much as possible of my relations. I then went on to Adelaide to finish loading, arriving there on the 18th June, and sailing again on the 21st. This being the off Wool season, the principal part of our cargo was Flour and wheat, with various sundries, such as Wine, Bark, and Hides, and we were booked to come home via the Cape of Good Hope, calling at Albany for Coal, arriving there on the 25th and leaving on the 26th June.

As this was the Winter season, I expected to get a dressing down from Westerly gales, but, on the whole, we did very well, far better than I expected, though we made a long passage home, and had to call into Las Palmas (Canary Islands) for Coal. I had often seen these Islands, but have only had the pleasure of calling at any of them on this one occasion. After coaling, we proceeded on our voyage, arriving In London on the 13th August, and at Liverpool on the 18th. The ship was dry-docked and coaled at the latter port, and then proceeded to Glasgow to load for Australia.

My stay home was very much broken up by coasting work, but my wife joined me in London and came round to Liverpool with us, this being the last time she made a trip in the Diomed.

While home off my first Australian voyage, my son, who had finished his apprenticeship, joined the S.S. Antenor as fifth engineer, making a voyage to China and back and then out to Australia ahead of me. On my arrival at Melbourne I met his ship, homeward bound, and the Captain kindly gave him a day off so that we might visit our friends together. But I am running ahead of my story, and must heave to and let it overhaul me or else I shall be in Irons, that being the expression used by old sailors to signify they were in a dilemma.

On the 31st August we sailed from Glasgow for Adelaide, passing the Cape of Good Hope on the twenty-fifth day out, but after leaving the Cape land, we found that our cylinders were passing steam and thus causing an increase in the consumption of coal. This necessitated our going into Albany for a further supply. Arriving there on the 14th October, we found one of our boilers leaking, which kept us a little longer than I expected, but we left with steam on the one boiler, and got the other to work a few hours after leaving. Arriving at Adelaide on the 19th October, we left again the same day, as we had but little cargo for that port. We were about three days in Melbourne, and it was here that I met my son and took him round to visit our relations, who all thought him a very fine young man. This was my last trip to Australia, but he has been two or three voyages since and I understand the Australian people are always very pleased to see him.

We arrived at Sydney on the 25th October, and of course, saw my sister and family. They were quite full of 'Jack', especially the girls, which I suppose is quite natural. From Sydney we went on to Brisbane, remaining there two days, discharging outward cargo and loading for London. We arrived back in Sydney on the 4th November, and left again for Melbourne on the 13th, remaining at the latter port two days, and then went on to a place called Portland to load a quantity of

Wool, then on to Kingston for about 2,000 bales.

Kingston Harbour, so called, is an open roadstead, and we lay about five miles off shore, the Wool being brought off by a small coasting steamer. Kingston is a very small place, and not often visited by large steamers. Many of the women-folk were desirous of seeing the 'big' ship, so the Captain of the coaster brought off about thirty women and children, telling them they would all be ashore by six in the evening. But he was a long way out in his reckoning, or, being an Irishman, did not stop to think that it was impossible to get the Wool discharged in so short a time, for in the first place, his crew had been working all night loading, and were well-nigh fagged out before he commenced, so the work went on very slowly, and as evening approached, it went slower still, finally dragging out until six o'clock next morning.

Of course the women folk were in great distress, and had to sit up all night, but we put the children into our bunks, and kept the ladies awake with hot Coffee. They were all tired out by morning, and I also, having been kept up to look after our visitors, felt like calling down, well, anything but blessings on the head of the impulsive Irishman who had placed me in such a predicament. I don't know what the ladies' husbands said to our friend, but I am sure the trip off to the Diomed was remembered in Kingston for many a long day.

We got away on the 23rd, arriving at Adelaide on the 24th, remaining there until the 29th November, sailing on that day for London via Suez Canal, making the passage to the Canal in 27 days 8 hours. Nothing happened worthy of note on the run, so after passing through the Canal—the portion of voyage I dislike very much—we proceeded on to London, arriving there on 10th January 1902. After paying off my crew I went down to Liverpool.

I omitted to mention that Mr Cable—the Chief Engineer—was not with us on this voyage, he having been transferred to the S.S. Antenor. Mr Hughes—the Chief Officer—had during our stay in Adelaide, come to an agreement with the stevedoring Company to come out and join them as what they termed 'Walking Foreman'. He thought it was a splendid opportunity of giving up the sea. Now I knew that our people were going to keep him back for Master after the current voyage, so I told him this, and strongly advised him not to act hastily, but his mind was made up to accept the shore job, one of his reasons being that he was afraid of being appointed to a Java ship, he having suffered so much from Fever. Judging from remarks he made from time to time, when discussing nautical matters with me, I came to the conclusion that the bad weather passage from Cardiff to Glasgow had tried his nerve so much, that he feared the responsibilities of Command might break him down. Poor fellow. He has now gone to his long home, but I can honestly and truthfully say he was a splendid officer and seaman, a good shipmate, and a gentleman from 'clew to earing', but his nerve was broken by the wretched Java fever.

I am a little in advance of my story in speaking of Mr Hughes' death, for later on, I shall have to mention him as being alive. With this explanation I will resume the thread of my narrative, by saying that in almost all the important changes occurring in my life, I have had a premonition beforehand, not a gloomy foreboding one, but just a feeling all over that a change was near. On this last voyage, when bidding the Australian friends Good-bye, I told them I feared it would be a long time before I came there again, and so strong was the feeling on the passage home, that I told my officers I thought it more than probable I would be transferred. Now I had no authority for saying what I did, but I had the courage of my convictions, and had all my gear packed up on arrival at London. I was therefore not at all surprised when the company's manager told me that they wished me to stay back and take Command of the S.S. Telemachus then building at Belfast. Doubtless most people will say this was merely a coincidence. Well, perhaps it was, but having had the feeling several times before, and never found it to miss fire, I may be excused if I do not agree with them.

Here, I may mention, that Mr Hughes resigned and went to Australia, and I had the pleasure of seeing both Messrs. Bebb and Wallace promoted, so the change was apparently a good one for us all.

About the 10th February 1902, I got into harness again, and was kept busy taking ships round the Coast until the 10th May, when I was sent over to Belfast to join the Telemachus. I found her a ship after my own heart, 4,802 tons register, and 7,749 tons Gross, 471 feet long and 54 feet beam. She steamed 13.8 knots on her trial trip, and could also carry 3,300 tons of water ballast, being in every respect, the finest type of cargo boat afloat, so I had every reason to feel proud of being her commander.

We left Belfast on the morning of the 15th May with Mr Workman, Mr Clark, and Mr G. Holt on board, also our own construction staff. After running the ship over the measured mile two or three times, and putting her through some manoeuvres, we had lunch, drinking the ship's health in Champagne. We then landed our Belfast friends and started out for Glasgow, experiencing thick dirty weather until we reached Greenock at 11 o'clock that night, anchoring there to wait for morning tide, then proceeding up to Glasgow and docking in Queen's Dock at 8 a.m. on the 16th May. After doing the necessary Customs' business, I went down that afternoon to Liverpool.

This finished another 'Jumping off' place in my life, or, as we sailors say, a fresh point of departure, so I think it would be better to start a fresh chapter with a new ship, but, before closing this one—which I fear will have proved dull reading to those who have read it—I would have them remember that this Memoir in no way claims to be a Novel, but simply a condensed history of my life, with a yarn or two thrown in.

A lady once asked me if I had ever been in a storm. I don't know what kind of a thing she had pictured to herself as a storm, but she was quite incredulous when I answered, "Plenty of them. Howling, shrieking, fiendish ones, such storms as the mind cannot picture, or the senses believe in until they have experienced one." In the same way my young readers will ask, "Were there no adventures, no exciting scenes, no Pirates or Slavers?" To such questions I may answer, "Plenty of adventures and excitement." But only once did I come into contact with Pirates, and that was after they were captured. We were then lying off the City of Whampoo, when a Chinese Gunboat brought in a big and noted Pirate Junk, and we used to have an armed boat nightly ahead and astern of us to keep off Pirates whilst lying at anchor at that port. As for Slavers, I have seen several of them after capture, and once I saw what may be considered an historical event connected with slavery, for it was the end of a very bad form of it, and as the story may prove interesting, I will relate it.

The Chincha islands, off the Coast of Peru, were noted for rich deposits of Guano, and many ships used to go there to load, but all very delayed for want of labour, so it struck some genius that there was plenty of human labour in China. Finding they could not get men by fair means, they started out to get them by foul, establishing for the purpose what they called 'Emigration Depots' at Macao, the only port owned in China by Portugal. The next thing was to get ships, and as no English vessel was allowed to enter into the trade, they bought about a dozen and fitted them up in an improved Slaver style, their tween decks being divided into three by iron grating bulkheads, and all round the sides of tween decks and amid-ships ran iron bars to fasten the refractory Chinamen to. There, Poops were fitted with an iron screen and guns were mounted and trained on the deck. The vessels used to arrive about June, and waited over the Typhoon season at Whampoo, Macao Harbour being much exposed.

During the time the ships were lying idle, the Agents were busy recruiting, *i.e.* buying, stealing, and inducing men to gamble away their liberty. All signed an indenture to serve ten years in the Chinchas. Those who would not sign voluntarily were beaten and starved until they did, and it was common knowledge the men were signing their death warrants, for no man was permitted to come back, and all worked under the control of the lash and revolver, both being used without fear or favour.

These facts were at last represented to the British Government, who protested strongly to both the Peruvian and Portuguese Governments, only to be met with an assurance that there could not possibly be any truth in the rumours, but they would look into the matter &c. The British did not lose any time arguing, but got after the Chinese Canton Government and persuaded them to order the withdrawal of the ships from Whampoo under pain of compulsion.

One fine day in July, orders came down from Canton that all the ships flying the Peruvian or Portuguese Flags were to leave Whampoo in 48 hours. Oh, what a commotion there was! None of them had full crews, no sails bent, and nothing ready. They hurriedly pulled down bulkheads and stowed away guns. The Captains went to the British Consul, telling him they were peaceful traders, and begging him to send his constable and British Captains to survey their ships, and see how innocent they were. They also pointed out that Whampoo was an open port, and it was an outrage on Europeans that surely Great Britain would not stand by and see committed. To this talk the British Consul replied, "Gentlemen, I have nothing to do with this matter. It is the Chinese government you must appeal to, or to your own Government at Macao. When the Chinese order a British ship to leave, I shall act, and do it promptly."

After 24 hours had expired, down came the Chinese War Junks, gongs beating, flags of all kinds flying, and guns firing. The Portuguese Captains were told that if the ships were not under way down the River when the 48 hours expired, they would be sunk. The first ebb after this notice was received, every ship was dropping down the River, accompanied by the War Junks, firing their guns and beating gongs. I don't know who were most afraid, the people in the ships, or War Junks, but a great factor in the case was two steam Gunboats, officered by Britishers, who stopped in the Beach above the Junks and followed slowly down after the others, apparently quite uninterested. This was the last of the slave traders. British influence in China was paramount in those days, but alas, its glory has departed. Yet, ask any Chinaman you meet from Shanghai to Java what white man he likes and trusts most, and he will answer, "More better that Englishman."

# Chapter 12

*1902 Maiden voyage in the Telemachus—Welsh coal to Nagasaki—holiday in Antwerp—brother Edward dies— meets old school chums—ship doctor drowns*

I introduced the S.S. Telemachus in the closing lines of my last chapter, and in continuation, may say that we sailed from Liverpool on June 1st 1902, bound for China and Japan. I found the ship most satisfactory in all respects, and having been in her for five years at the time of writing this chapter, I can truthfully say that the opinion I then formed still stands good. There is an old saying, that next to his wife a sailor loves his ship best. I don't go quite so far as that, but I do say he gets to feel every confidence in a vessel, and is, as the Spiritualists say, in rapport with her. I don't know how that sort of a traverse works, but I do think there is on some points, a stronger connection between the animate and inanimate than is allowed for in an ordinary course and distance.

Telemachus, on this her maiden passage, was initiated into the perils of the sea and the mighty forces of the elements by running into the Southern edge of a Typhoon in the China Sea. I hauled her to the S.E. for a time, and then gradually worked up behind the disturbance. Of course, we got some dirty weather, but came up smiling for the next round.

We arrived at Yokohama in due course, and commenced to load home on the London and Antwerp berth. After calling at Kobe, and on our passage through the Inland Sea, we encountered a Typhoon, but were able to reach an anchorage under a place called Miya Saki. It blew and rained hard all night, the centre passing over us at about 4 a.m. The shift was a moderate one, and it rapidly fined up, so we got under way at 6 a.m. and at 11 a.m. we fell in with a water-logged Japanese Schooner, and rescued the only survivor of her crew, the others having been washed away and drowned during the night (August 11th 1902).

In continuation of our voyage, we called at Shanghai and Colombo, and then on to London, Antwerp, and Liverpool, arriving at the latter port October 18th 1902.

On November 5th I received orders to take my ship to Barry and load 4,000 tons of Coal for Nagasaki. From Barry we went to Glasgow and Liverpool, sailing from the latter port for China and Japan on November 21st. On our passage through the Suez Canal, we took the ground heavily with our starboard forward bilge. I feared damage below the water line, but she showed no signs of leaking, so I proceeded on my voyage, nothing happening until the night after passing Perim, when we encountered a smart breeze and head sea from the E.S.E. This made the ship jump about considerably, but no thought of danger entered my mind, and my astonishment and dismay can be realised, when at daylight we found 13 feet of water in the No. 1 Lower Hold. Fortunately this hold was three-quarters full of coal, so after getting the pumps to work, which overcame the inflow of water, we got down into the hold, and dug down to the starboard bilge, out through the floor and got into the bilge where we found the bracket frames twisted up and the outer plating in the same condition. We effected makeshift repairs, and I caused a six inch hole to be cut into the side of No. 1 ballast tank, so that if the leak overpowered the deck pumps, the water would run into the tank, and be dealt with by the tank steam pumps.

We then proceeded on our voyage to Singapore and there discharged some of the coal, and filled the bilge up solid with concrete, thus making the ship seaworthy and fit to carry a dry, perishable cargo.

I am however forging ahead of my story, for our troubles were not yet over, as while lying at the Shanghai Wharf, a fire broke out in our No. 4 tween decks, which did considerable damage before it was got under. Well, we are all born to trouble as the sparks fly upward. Ours flew up and went out, so our troubles passed away.

We loaded home on the Amsterdam and London berth, calling at Marseilles on the way, and arriving in London on March 30th 1903.

On my going down to Liverpool, the Owners told me we were to make the next voyage across the Pacific, and for a start we were to go to Antwerp and load 8,000 tons of rails and 1,000 tons of Firebricks for Pacific ports. From Antwerp we were to come on to Liverpool, so seeing it was nice Spring weather at home, I took my wife and daughter Meg with me, and we got ten beautiful (?) winter days in Antwerp. When it was not snowing, it was hailing, or else it was miserably wet and cold. However, it was a beautiful day leaving, and we had a fine passage to Liverpool, sailing from there again on May 1st.

Our route on this Pacific voyage was via Colombo, Penang, Singapore, Hong Kong, Nagasaki, Moji, Kobe, Yokohama, Victoria [Texas], Vancouver, Seattle and Tacoma [Washington state]. This as will be readily seen, gave us a sufficiently wide range of ports to make the voyage an interesting one from a traveller's point of view, but the voyage was to be still more interesting before we finished, for it proved to be the longest voyage I have ever made in a steamer. We arrived at Victoria on July 6th 1903, but the charm of the place—for it is a charming place in summer—was taken away by the sad news I received of my brother Edward's death, which took place suddenly on the 7th of June in Glasgow. He was buried in Craighorn Cemetery, on the Paisley Road, my daughter Carrie attending the funeral on my behalf. Poor dear Ted! He had many years of pain and trouble both in the body and spirit, but he bore his troubles well, trusting in his Heavenly Father always, and humbly following in the footsteps of Jesus. He was very dear to me, and his death caused much sorrow to all who knew him.

The evening of my arrival I went for a stroll—the ship lying practically in the Country—and on my return at about 8 o'clock, the Quartermaster on duty at the gangway told me that a gentleman—then on board— had been enquiring for me and asking if I belonged to Liverpool, and if my name was John. On asking what he had told the gentleman, he replied, "I thought your name was George, and that you were Scotch, because you had a brother in Glasgow."

While thus talking to the Quartermaster, he said to me, "The gentleman is now coming along the deck, Sir." Looking up I saw a man coming quickly towards me with his hand stretched out and an eager delighted look on his face, which latter I knew, but could not fix. Reaching me, he grasped my hand and shook it with a will, exclaiming, "I knew it was you, John, as soon as I saw you."

"Well," I replied, "your face is familiar, but I cannot give you a name."

"What," he replied, "you don't know John Nixon?"

Then my eyes were opened, and I knew him for an old school-fellow and particular chum, whom I had not seen for 38 years.

"Well," I said, "Jack, I am right down glad to see you again, and you must forgive me for not knowing you, but I had no idea you were in this part of the World, so you had the advantage of me. But, how did you know I was here?"

"I did not," he replied, "but being in Victoria on business, I picked up the evening paper at the Hotel and saw in the shipping news, Telemachus from Liverpool, Goodwin, Master, so I wondered if that was Jack Goodwin, my old chum, and I trotted down to see, but hardly expecting it was you."

He told me be was living in Vancouver with his family, consisting of a wife, three boys and five girls, and that he was a Contractor and was then in Victoria getting timber concessions located up Barkley Sound.

He further told me he was returning home in two days.

"Well," I said, "we are sailing for Vancouver the day after to-morrow, why not come with us?"

To this he agreed, and on our arrival at Vancouver his eldest son met us and after I had done my business and put everything in working order, I went on to Jack's home and saw his eldest daughter, his wife and the young ones, being in the woods on a Summer Camp. It was arranged that as I was to be in Vancouver until the following Tuesday, we—that is, John Nixon, his son, daughter, and myself—should sail over to where the family were on the Saturday and stay until Monday morning. This we did, and I spent a most enjoyable time, partly on the shore and in the backwoods with trees 200 feet high all round us, and at night sleeping in a tent. I don't know that I ever spent a pleasanter time in my life, and was quite in love with Vancouver. Having been there several times since, I still have the same opinion of it, and think there is a big future before British Columbia, and it is coming to the front fast. In due course, and with much regret, I left Vancouver, and my friends, proceeding to Seattle to discharge the balance of our cargo.

I found the latter place a thriving busy town, but somehow I was not taken with it. Vancouver had probably spoiled me, but as a matter of fact Seattle is neither American, English, nor Continental, and, so mixed in the population, you feel as if every other one you meet would address you in High Dutch or Italian, so I was not sorry to leave it and go on to Tacoma. There it was quieter and much more to my liking, a great number of the inhabitants being British born. They of course have become American Citizens, but never forget the 'Old Country'. Their children for the most part are Americans pure and simple, and rightly so. They are taught at school to be Americans and to love and honour the Flag which they call 'Old Glory'. We don't do that kind of thing in England. In fact of late, cases have occurred in which Managers of Board Schools have refused to hoist the British Flag over their schools on the grounds that it teaches militarism. They are 'Little Englanders' who one and all deserve 'keelhauling'.

The ship remained in Tacoma for 21 days loading 2½ million feet of Timber for the American Government at Manila. We also loaded a quantity of timber for Yokohama, Kobe, and Hong Kong, sailing from Tacoma on the 9th August and arriving at Hong Kong on the 5th September. At the latter port I received orders to proceed to Java from Manila for homeward loading. This was giving us a change of scenery with a vengeance. We arrived at Manila on the 12th September 1903, and found it a very interesting place, but being rapidly Americanised. What struck me most was the number of American Civilians in the place, and the thought that occurred to me was, if there are so many openings in the U.S. America for foreign Emigrants, why on earth do so many Americans have to go abroad for their living?

We left Manila on the 24th September and arrived in Batavia 2nd October, just ten years since I last visited it. From Batavia we went right round the Island of Java, visiting Indramayo, Samarang, Sourabaya, Pasocrocan, Probolingo, and Panaruken, thence back to Indramayo and Batavia, from which latter port we sailed for home via Jeddah with 280 Pilgrims. We put into Colombo for Coal, and found our rudder needed some repairs, which took five days to execute. We then proceeded on our voyage, landed our passengers at Jeddah, and then on to the Canal and Port Said, from which port we sailed on the 30th November. We experienced bad weather in the Mediterranean, and called at Gibraltar for Coal, finally arriving at Amsterdam on the 16th December, and at London on the 21st, having been 7 months and 21 days on the voyage.

We left London on the 24th December 1903, for Liverpool, thus missing the only possible chance I had of being home for Christmas Day for ten years. We had a beautiful passage round the Coast—indeed it was more like summer than winter, and I enjoyed the family gathering which always takes place at my home on New Year's Day.

We sailed for Newport on the 16th January and after loading 5,000 tons of Coal for Nagasaki, returned to Liverpool to finish loading with general cargo for our usual ports of call on the China-Japan route, sailing from Liverpool 30th January 1904.

While at home my step-mother—Mrs J. M. Goodwin— died, aged about 80 years, and was buried in Anfield Cemetery, Walton. I had not seen her for 30 years, but I attended her funeral at the request of her nephew and my friend, Mr George Rose.

The War had now broken out between Japan and Russia, so our coal was declared for the use of the British Government, who had a coal depot at Nagasaki, but as a matter of fact the Japanese got 4,000 tons of it, and the British the rest. After discharging we proceeded on our voyage to Yokohama, and there commenced to load home on the Amsterdam-London berth, calling at Kobe, at which port I always receive a warm welcome from my friends—the Devenishes. We arrived at Shanghai on the 15th April 1904, and I was there advised that we were to take 300 Naval Ratings from Hong Kong to Plymouth. Well, to cut the yarn short, I embarked the ratings, also about 15 Soldiers from Singapore, and landed them in Plymouth on the 14th June.

I must say I was amused with our people over the carrying of the Naval Ratings, for on the voyage I carried them in the Diomed it took the whole Liverpool and Birkenhead staff to get the ship ready in a week for 400 men, and then the Governors impressed upon me the vast importance of getting a good report from the Commanding Officer, and after our return home with a good one, they made me a present of £25, and the officers a month's extra pay. In the last instance, I had four days to fit up quarters and provision for 300 men, superintending all myself, and when I reached home they never as much as mentioned that I had carried troops, maintaining a discreet silence.

From Plymouth we proceeded to Amsterdam, and being informed there that the Dutch Government were granting Certificates of Service to shipmasters who could prove service in Dutch vessels, I applied for one, and after undergoing medical examination, I was granted a Certificate as Master in the Dutch Mercantile Marine, though I did not receive it for 16 months afterwards. This was owing to my not being in Amsterdam during that time.

From Amsterdam we went to London, Glasgow, and Liverpool, loading outwards for China, Japan, and Vancouver, finally sailing from Liverpool 23rd July 1904. We arrived at Colombo 17th August, and whilst there I received a letter from my friend Captain Lowry, telling me it had been arranged that himself and wife, also a Mr Weir from the Singapore office, were to come as passengers with me to Vancouver.

We left Singapore on the 28th August 1904, and after calling at usual ports, we arrived at Yokohama on the 19th September. Now the Russo-Japan War was still going on, and the Russian Cruiser Fleet had been making raids on Japanese ships, and neutral vessels carrying what they—the Russians—considered contraband of war, and one of our Company's steamers had had to land a lot of railway material consigned to Hakodate at Yokohama, and the Russians having for the time being been driven into Vladivostock, I was ordered to take the stuff on to Hakodate. This I did, arriving there safely on the 27th September, and after due discharge proceeded to a place called Mororan, in the Island of Yesso, for coaling purposes. The two last mentioned ports were new to myself and friends, and the weather being fine, we enjoyed our visits very much, leaving on 30th September for Victoria, B.C., at which port we arrived after a passage of 14 days 10 hours, proceeding in due course to Vancouver and arriving there 15th October. My passengers left me at this port and went across to New York via the Canadian Pacific Railway, just a little late in the season for the trip, but they afterwards told me they had a most enjoyable trip across the American Continent, but the weather was very cold.

At Vancouver we loaded some 90,000 cases of Salmon for London and Liverpool, and then proceeded to Seattle and Tacoma to finish loading. We left Tacoma 27th October, calling at Victoria for passengers, of which we took 100 Japs and Chinese. Our passage over was a very rough one, taking us nearly 19 days to Yokohama, and on arrival I was advised that we loaded homewards on the London berth. We also heard that the Company's steamer Calchas had been captured and taken to Vladivostock. She was on her passage from Tacoma to Yokohama with Flour and was seized by a Russian Cruiser only 50 miles from Yokohama. Truly there is many a slip between the cup and the lip. The Russian Cruiser also found this proverb true, for she was really looking for a San Francisco liner with a million pounds of Specie on board for the Japanese Government. A dense fog prevailed and when it lifted the treasure ship was just far enough up the Tokio Gulf to be under the protection of the Jap Forts, and our ship close to the Cruiser.

Nothing worthy of record occurred during the remainder of this voyage, which terminated in London on the 22nd January 1905.

I had a very good holiday, but the weather was very cold, so I spent a good deal of the time by the fireside. Shortly before sailing again, I received a letter from my friend, Captain Lowry, telling me that it had been arranged for them to go out to Singapore with me. I was greatly pleased to hear this news, and in due time they came to Liverpool and made the acquaintance of my wife and family, both parties being mutually pleased with each other.

We sailed on the 5th March, and after calling at the usual ports, including Singapore, where I landed my passengers, we arrived at Victoria on the 20th May, proceeding thence to Vancouver, at which port my friends—the Nixons—gave me a warm welcome. We loaded in Tacoma and came home on the usual run to Hong Kong only deviating to call at Mororan for Coal. At Hong Kong I received orders to go to Java for homeward loading and after visiting various ports finally sailed from Batavia on the 23rd August for Suez, Marseilles, Amsterdam and Liverpool.

I am however running ahead of my story, for the day after leaving Tacoma, my Chief Engineer brought me a Liverpool paper, in which was the announcement of my son's marriage. This was confirmed by letter from my wife at Yokohama. It appears he got married quietly at the Registry Office on the 7th January 1905, while I was home, and still lived at home, saying nothing, but on being appointed to the S.S. Antenor as third engineer, and she being ordered to Swansea for outward loading, he could not think of being there for 14 days without seeing his wife, so they avowed their marriage. His mother was very much upset and insisted on them being married again in Church, his wife's parents also concurring. It was this marriage I saw in the paper. I met my son in Shanghai on July 20th, and he gave me his reasons for acting as he had done, and I was quite satisfied that the reasons he gave were good and pure.

I may mention that he had passed his examination for Chief Engineer just before his marriage.

While at Sourabaya on this voyage, a sad accident occurred. Our Doctor—Mr J. Soutter—having no Dutch Medical Certificate, was transferred to the S.S. Pyrrhus on account of our carrying Dutch Javanese Pilgrims to Jeddah, and on the transfer being arranged, he came on shore with me to the Consulate for the usual business. Whilst there he asked if he could have the day to take a run up the railway line and see the country. His request having been granted, I bid him goodbye, cautioning him at the same time to be very careful if he went off to his new ship after dark, as a strong tide would be running against a contrary wind.

Well, to be brief, he went off in a native boat about midnight. I was on deck at the time, and saw the boat making for the S.S. Pyrrhus. It was bright moonlight, and as the tide was running about five knots against a strong wind, I watched the little craft anxiously until she was alongside the vessel, then, seeing her sail come down, felt she was all right, though I did not then know Dr Soutter was in her. A little later I saw her leave the ship's side, and as she drifted towards us the sail was hoisted, and the boat headed for the shore. Next morning I learned that Dr Soutter was in her, and when trying to get on the gangway ladder he missed his hold, fell overboard, and was never seen again. Nor were we able to trace the boat, but the Quartermaster on the gangway saw all that happened. Poor Soutter, he was a fine fellow, and his death cast quite a gloom over us.

As before mentioned, we sailed from Batavia on the 23rd August 1905, and arrived at Jeddah on the 10th September, sailing thence for Marseilles and Amsterdam, arriving at the latter port on the 1st October. At Amsterdam I was relieved by Captain Parkinson (afterwards the survivor of the Berlin disaster) who took the ship to Liverpool and Glasgow, the Chief Officer— Mr Smart—bringing her to Liverpool, whence I rejoined her in due course.

And so having brought my readers thus far, I will conclude this Chapter, and come to anchor until the spirit moves me to write again.

# Chapter 13

*1905 Liverpool—Bessie's debut in St George's hall—*
*fifty-seventh birthday at home—first grandson born—*
*family reunion—Japan*

Being in the humour to continue my history—for one must be in a good vein to do so—I give a hitch to my pants, turn over my quid 'sailor fashion' and start off with a free wind and flowing sail.

I left Liverpool in the S.S. Telemachus on November 11th 1905, bound to China, Japan, and the Pacific Coast, but before proceeding further, should mention that Mr Smart, my Chief Officer, had left owing to trouble with his Eyesight, and Mr J. Bebb, my old Diomed officer, joined me as Chief. We arrived in due course at Yokohama, and left again on January 16th, experiencing a very rough passage across the Pacific, Easterly gales, snow and hard frost prevailing all the way. We did the usual ports on the Sound, and took in a new one—Union Bay, in Baynes Sound [British Colombia].

Arriving at Tacoma on February 12th, 1906, we loaded for Japan (calling for coal at Mororan), China, and home, reaching Amsterdam May 11th, and London May 14th. At the latter port I was relieved, and my ship after calling at Antwerp, Liverpool, and Glasgow, finally arrived in Liverpool, for outward loading on June 17th. I then rejoined her and sailed on June 23rd 1906, on the same run as last voyage, with the addition of one new port called Keelung in the North end of Formosa, at which place we loaded 300 tons Tea and 200 tons Sulphur for America.

This voyage our sailings on Puget Sound were altered, and from Victoria we went to Tacoma and Seattle, thence to Vancouver, and Union Bay, and back again to Seattle and Tacoma, finally sailing from the last named on October 4th. After calling at Victoria for passengers, we proceeded on to Yokohama, arriving there October 22nd 1906. Here I was advised that we were to load homewards on the Liverpool berth. We called at the usual China ports, Singapore, Jeddah, Genoa and Marseilles, and arrived at Liverpool on January 9th 1907. Genoa was a new port to me, and I found it a very interesting place, but rapidly being modernised. On arriving at Liverpool, my owners advised me that they were taking my ship out of the Pacific run, and intended for the future to run her in the China and Japan trade. Now although I had been complaining about the long voyages across the Pacific, with the contrariness of human nature, I felt sorry about the change. Perhaps, because I had made many friends in Vancouver, for I don't know any other reason, and, as a matter of fact, I should have been glad, for the new departure would give me much more time at home, and I can assure my readers that at the present time I have no wish to go back into the Pacific trade.

Whilst at home my daughter Bessie—who had established herself as a teacher of Elocution, and for business purposes was a member of an Amateur Dramatic Club—made her début at St. George's Hall in a piece called 'The Cape Mail', she taking one of the principal characters. Of course the family turned up in force, and we all were very proud of her ability and talent. I won't say too much, because I may be thought biased, she without doubt being the family favourite.

After a very pleasant stay at home, I again sailed on February 10th 1907, for Penang, Singapore, Hong Kong, and Shanghai, and on arrival at latter port was instructed to go to a place in Japan called Kuchinotsu for Coal, and then proceed to Saigon, Cochin China, and load a full cargo of Rice Meal for Liverpool. This was indeed a change, and a very agreeable one. Both ports were new to me, and I was much interested with what I saw in both places. After completing our loading at Saigon, we sailed on April 29th for Liverpool, via Singapore and Canal, arriving at the former port on June 4th 1907.

This gave me my 57th birthday at home. I don't know that I was much the better for that, excepting always the loving pleasure it gave my wife and daughters, not forgetting myself. I may say it does not matter how long one is home from a voyage, the sailing day seems to come rapidly on again, and hardened old salt that I am, the parting from my dear wife is a great sorrow, which does not tend to grow less as time goes on. My wife is a brave little woman, God bless her, and never makes a fuss, but I know her heart weeps in silence. Verily a good wife is a crown of joy to her husband, and her children shall rise up and call her blessed.

Returning to my story, I may add that we sailed from Liverpool on July 5th 1907, for the Straits, China and

Japan, and with the exception of a very strong Monsoon in the Arabian Sea, we did not experience any untoward incidents, arriving at our ports in due course and once again visiting a new port in Japan, called Tokoyama, taking there some 500 tons of Pitch for the Japanese Patent Fuel Factory established at that port. The town is an ordinary Japanese one, and did not create any great amount of interest in any of us. After due discharge of our cargo, we proceeded to Kobe and Yokohama, reaching the latter on September 4th.

Whilst at Kobe, I received a letter from my wife, informing me of the birth of a Grandson, who was born at 10.20 p.m. on Tuesday, 23rd July 1907. He was christened at St. Phillip's Church, Litherland, being named 'Leslie John Royce Goodwin'. Leslie, to please his mother, John after his father and grandfather, and Royce to please his maternal grandparents. I was delighted with the little fellow when I saw him, and without doubt he is the best tempered baby I ever came across, and if he goes on being as good tempered, he will fulfil the old prophesy, that 'a Tuesday's child is full of grace'.

Of course the female part of the family differ as to who he is like in the face, but all agree that the back of his head is mine in shape and expression.

Naturally, I was amused at this, until I saw him, and was then simply amazed at the likeness, the more so as his father has but little resemblance to me.

Now I will have to take a reef in my topsails, and haul closer to the wind on my story tack. I have no doubt my readers will understand what I mean, though, alas, the days of reefs have almost passed away.

At Yokohama we commenced to load on the London, Amsterdam, and Antwerp berth, and sailing on September 10th arrived at Shanghai on the 16th, and from there were ordered to Foochow, arriving on September 21st, after an absence from this port of eight years. After loading some 500 tons of Tea, we proceeded on our voyage to Hong Kong, Singapore, Penang, Colombo, and London, at which port I was relieved for holiday and did not rejoin my ship until November 29th at Glasgow, where we were detained two days by fog, sailing on December 2nd for Liverpool and arriving next day. I found my dear wife and daughters quite well, and the former very much improved in health. I also had the pleasure of seeing my son, who was at home when I got there from London, his ship the Orestes—of which he is second engineer—sailing for Australia somewhere about the 22nd November.

My sister Eleanor came over from Belfast under very sad circumstances. Her husband, who had been sailing on the China and Japan Coast for some 14 years, was sent home as an invalid, and on his arrival in London was in a dazed condition. He lost himself and was found in a place called Leytonstone, and was taken to Hospital, his identity being established by a letter on his person. After being in hospital for a week he died, his wife having reached him two days before his death, which was a happy release for him and her. I am sorry to have to say this, but facts are stubborn things.

I also heard from my sister Annie, who lives near Liverpool, Sydney, Australia, and I gathered from her letter that she was keeping her end up. My cousin,

John M. Goodwin, of Melbourne also wrote me. He is my brother Edward's type, physically, but mine in disposition.

And now I must return to my present voyage. I say present, because I have brought my memoirs up to date, so what I write will be more of a daily record but, should the spirit move me later, I may write a chapter of Yarns and personal experiences, which may serve to amuse those who take the trouble to read what I have written.

We sailed from Liverpool on December 8th 1907, and experienced very bad weather up to Cape St. Vincent. As our coal had been cut short on account of cargo, we had to go into Algiers for a further supply. Thus I renewed my acquaintance with this port after an absence of more than eight years. I saw very little change in the place, except that the town had extended. From Algiers we went on to Port Said, only to find a coal Strike prevailing, so we had to take in sufficient with our crew to take us to Perim. We had our Christmas Day in the Red Sea, and a very pleasant day it was as far as weather was concerned, and I congratulated myself on being where I was, instead of in England with its cold, bleak weather. We arrived in Perim on December 28th, and, as with Algiers, I renewed my acquaintance after an absence of over eight years. I found it still the same barren, dreary place, though the Manager of the Coal Company told me they had a few green things on the Island. These I think they must keep under a glass case.

Returning to business, I may say that a Coal Strike at Port Said means a Coal famine at Perim so I was not surprised to learn that they could not supply all the

Coal I wanted, but only enough to enable me to reach Colombo, so I had to be content and make my way there, arriving on January 5th, after a boisterous passage for the time of the year. We arrived at Singapore on January 13th, and sailed on the 14th. This being the N.E. Monsoon season, and they being reported very strong, I determined to take the route outside Formosa, and so get into the Japan current. This was a success until we were about abreast of the North end of the Island when it came down a howling black North-Easter, with bitter cold weather. So sudden was the change that we were wearing tropical clothes until 4 p.m. and by 8 p.m. we had on our winter ones. However, these changes have to be endured, and form part of a sailor's life.

We arrived at Shanghai on January 27th, and after discharging the cargo for that port, went on to Nagasaki, Moji, Kobe, and Yokohama, arriving at the latter port on February 6th. We sailed again on the 9th for Shanghai, loading homewards on the Genoa, Marseilles, and Liverpool berth. We left Shanghai on February 18th for Hong Kong, at which port we took on board some 400 Chinese passengers for Singapore. We made a good passage to the latter port, and after taking in 6,000 tons of cargo, we went on to Penang to finish our homeward loading, sailing thence on the 6th March for Suez, arriving there in due course, and after passing through the Canal we sailed for Genoa on the 23rd, and arrived on the 28th March. We stayed in Genoa about four days, and I saw a great deal of the town and its surroundings, and the more I saw of it, the better I liked the place, it being one of the most interesting towns I have ever seen. From Genoa we went on to Marseilles, and thence on to Liverpool, arriving home on the 10th April 1908, and found all well.

# Chapter 14

*1908 Reminiscences—pilgrims to Jeddah—old Irish yarn—
the S.S. Great Eastern—man overboard—Hindoo burning
grounds—more yarns—rainmaking in Cheyenne*

During my stay at home I, accompanied by my wife
and daughters—Carrie and Bessie—paid a visit to
Newcastle, County Down, Ireland, and spent a week
there with my friends, Captain and Mrs Lowry, and
despite the fact that we had snow for three days, rain
for two, and very indifferent weather the other two days
of our stay, we enjoyed our visit very much.

We returned to Liverpool on the 1st of May, and on
the next day I sailed in my ship to Newport, Mon.,
accompanied by my wife, and on our arrival, we
secured very nice apartments ashore, staying there a
week. The country around Newport is very fine and I
looked forward to some nice strolls with my wife, but
unfortunately it rained best part of the time and thus
spoiled our plans, but we had a pleasant and happy
time.

After loading some 3,000 tons of Coal, and various
other cargo, we sailed for Liverpool on the 9th of May
and after an all too short week at home I sailed for
China and Japan on the 16th of May.

I regret to say that while in Newport I heard from
Newcastle to the effect that my friend, Mrs Lowry, had
been thrown from a Motor Car, and badly injured, but

was pleased to learn by a letter from Captain Lowry at Port Said that she was improving and hoped to be about again in a couple of weeks.

While home, I had my first experience of what most fathers of grown-up daughters have to go through—that is, being asked for the hand of one of their daughters. This refers to Meg, the second girl. It was not unexpected, but I confess I felt upset when my permission was asked, and the poor mother was more than upset. Why should this be so, I wonder? The man she is to marry is in every way desirable, and we are glad to see her settled, but I suppose the truth is, we don't want to lose her, and it seems too much like the breaking up of our hitherto happy family life.

We arrived at our various China ports in due course, and then proceeded to Kuchinotsu and Moji in Japan. At the latter port, my friend, Captain Devenish, joined us as inland Sea Pilot to Kobe, but we unfortunately discovered a hitherto unknown sand-bank on which we stranded at 11 a.m. July 5th, remaining aground for 35 hours, during which time we discharged 2,000 tons of cargo, after which we came off practically undamaged, and proceeded on our way to Kobe and Yokohama. At the latter port, we remained a week, and then started to load homewards on the Marseilles-Havre and Liverpool berth, calling at Saigon for cargo, and at Singapore and Penang. Also at the two last named ports, in addition to cargo, we took on board 1,100 Pilgrims for Jeddah, sailing from Penang on the 17th August 1908.

After a fairly moderate Monsoon, we arrived at Kamaran [largest island in mouth of Red Sea] on the 31st of August, having had only one death on the passage, but two more pilgrims died while at the Quarantine Station.

On the 4th of September we re-embarked our pilgrims and proceeded to Jeddah, arriving on the 6th of September. We found Jeddah very hot. Indeed some of my boys described it as 'a little Hell' and I quite agreed with them. Nevertheless I, for the first time in my life, went ashore to see the town, which was very interesting, but like all Turkish places [Jeddah then in the Ottoman Empire] it is in a state of decay, and owing to a 'Constitution' having lately been granted in Turkey, the Turkish soldiers in Jeddah—numbering about 60 men—revolted, and put the Governor in jail, and a Committee of town Arabs and soldiers were running the place. In the meantime the Bedouin Arabs were gathered outside the City, threatening to attack it. Telegraph communication was cut off, and the foreign Consuls were putting the Consulates into a state of defence, and I, on the point of sailing—on the 9th of September— was entrusted with despatches to the French, Dutch, Russian, and English Governments, asking for help in the shape of Gunboats. There is a wall round Jeddah, but as far as I was able to judge it would not keep out any determined body of soldiers—it being in a state of decay, and not one cannon to defend it.

We arrived at Suez on the 12th of September, and left Port Said on the 13th, arriving at Marseilles on the 19th, and left for Havre on the 21st, and after a stay of 24 hours, in Havre, we proceeded to Liverpool, arriving there on 1st October, and found all well.

*Come all you jolly sailors bold,*
*And listen unto me,*
*And tales to you I will unfold,*
*Tales of the Sea.*

I promised in the course of my writings to tell some of the incidents of my life, or some of the things I have seen from time to time. They will necessarily be told just as they occur to my mind, without regard to sequence.

I have always been keenly interested in the History and Politics of my Country, and being home on the Hundredth Anniversary of the Battle of Trafalgar I felt proud that in my younger days I had talked with several men who were in the battle, also soldiers of Waterloo. One man named Simmons, who had been a privateersman and also a Man-of-Warsman at Trafalgar I used to look on with great awe. He died in the year 1860, aged 86, and his old wife took me in to see him as he lay before they put him in his coffin. The old lady herself used to tell some hair-raising yarns about ghosts. She was a Manx woman, and very superstitious, and told me the following yarn of herself.

In her village there was a superstition that if a drowned person was lying in the Church awaiting burial, and a young person at the dead of night went into the Church and put a cross with chalk on the coffin, he or she, would never be drowned. Well, she did this when 18 years old, and I know she was not drowned, for I saw her on her deathbed. But I doubt very much if the little incident mentioned proved a talisman in her life. She was an active old party to the last, and not averse to a pull on an old black clay pipe. She died when 84 years of age.

An old lady—a Mrs Holmes of Dublin—deeply interested me with tales of the Irish Rebellion of 1790. This was in 1862, she being then over 90 years of age, bedridden, but with faculties clear and bright. She knew my Grandfather Goodwin and I have regretted since that I did not learn more of him from her.

I remember when the first Atlantic cable [telegraph] was laid by two men-of-war Steam Frigates, and the disappointment when the cable failed to act after almost the first message. Then the Great Eastern came along to make the next attempt.

What a marvel we thought she was, with her seven masts and five funnels, and she was a 'marvel' of ship-building for those days, but far before her time. She really was unmanageable in heavy weather, principally on account of the want of power to control her steering. She had eight wheels on one long spindle, and she took sixteen men, one each side the wheels, and even then in bad weather she has thrown them in all directions, even killing some. My father took me on board of her in New York in 1861, going off to her in a sailing boat. Three things impressed me very much. Firstly, the man in charge of the boat was a down-East Yankee, and he had his mouth full of Tobacco, which he accidentally swallowed. I don't think I ever saw a sicker man in my life, and the memory of it kept me from any desire to chew Tobacco. Secondly, I heard my father say to another Captain who was with us, referring to the 'Great Eastern', "Yes, she is a big ship, but if you and I live for another twenty years, ships of her size will be common." He was not far out, though it took a little longer than that before his prediction came true. Thirdly, the ship's immense size as compared with the then crack Atlantic liner Persia which was lying close to her, impressed me very much, and I can see the contrast in my mind's eye after 47 years have come and gone as plainly as I saw it then. There was intense interest and excitement in Liverpool while she was laying the Atlantic Cable, and when communication ceased quite a gloom was cast over the Kingdom, and the disappointment was great when the news came that the Cable was broken and lost.

After that, I lost interest in her, and though I saw her often afterwards, I never gave her much thought, until I saw her on Rock Ferry beach [Birkenhead] being broken up for old Iron. My thought then was, "Alas, how are the mighty fallen." R.I.P.

Some will think it strange and a little eerie that on two occasions, both being on dark nights, we lost a man overboard from the old ship Comorin. Both times I was at the Wheel, steering, and on the Captain rushing on deck, when the awful cry "Man overboard" rang out, it was reported to be me that had gone. The first time the Captain was near enough for me to sing out, "No, it's not me, Sir." The second time they reported it was me I did not hear them, and one can imagine the Captain's blank amazement when he walked aft, giving at the same time an order to the man at the wheel, my stentorian voice answered in the usual way, "Luff it is, Sir," or whatever the order was. He peered in my face for a moment and then said. "Thank God, lad. It was not you, they told me it was." (I was, by-the-way, a great favourite of his.) Nothing could be done to save the poor fellow from the maintop-gallant yard while furling the sail. I shall never forget his awful cry when he fell and the sickening thud when his body struck the rail and rolled overboard. But enough of such sad subjects.

My first acquaintance with a submarine earthquake was in the year 1866. This occurred while near the Equator, and about 22° West Longitude. It made the ship quiver and shake from stem to stern for quite a minute, and we reeled to and fro on her decks like drunken men, and were all jolly well scared. I have often experienced these seaquakes since, but never such a severe one.

I have no doubt my readers will remember my being in the ship Arracan. Well, in the year 1867 she was dismasted in a Cyclone whilst lying at anchor off Sangor, at the entrance of the Hooghly. She was towed back to Calcutta, and dry-docked for repairs, lying in dock two months. Now she had 14 Apprentices, and a wild lot they were. The Chief Officer used to try and keep their noses to the grindstone, and they used to set their wits to work and endeavour to get the weather gauge of him. There were two fine pigs on board, and a bright idea struck one of the lads that if the pigs got ashore, they would be sent to look for them, so the sty door was opened at night, and the grunters had disappeared in the morning. The mate was much concerned, as the Captain was having the Pigs fattened for his use at home, so off all the boys started and neither they nor the pigs were seen for three days. Some of the lads came on board our ship and told us what a time they were having, but none of them had reckoned on the sequel.

Not very far from the ship was the Hindoo burning ground for their dead, whose horrors I tried to describe in the earlier part of my memoirs. Now the pigs found their way there, and revelled in dead men's bones, &c., and as pigs must eat, I can leave my readers to surmise what happened. Anyway the lads saw quite enough for their stomachs, and they were a meek lot when they drove those pigs on board, enduring the mate's abuse and punishment with such exemplary patience and meekness, that he wanted to know what Missionary Society they had joined in their absence. The boys kept their own counsel as to burning grounds.

However, on the passage home one of the pigs was killed, owing to shortage of provisions, but not one of the crowd partook thereof, preferring to go hungry. Surely the ways of transgressors are hard. I knew all the lads well—indeed one of them was my chum—and he told me the sequel some time after, but he had not then recovered from his dislike to fresh pork.

The Arracan and Comorin were sister ships and on that particular voyage there were 14 of us apprentices in each ship—28 in all—and at this day I am the sole survivor. All have gone to their long home. Truly I can say, "What am I, that God in his mercy should have spared me and taken so many?"

One voyage in the Comorin we got ashore on the notorious James & Mary's quicksands in the river Hooghly. We had a very narrow escape from turning turtle, and a boat's crew, including myself, had a still narrower escape while carrying out an anchor. We were in the long boat—now a thing of the past—and while paying out the cable, it took charge of us, and rip it went to the end on the anchor, which was hanging on the boat's stern, and down went her stern under water. But for the prompt action of my old friend, Bob Nelson, who, having an axe in his hand, quickly cut the slip rope and the boat righted three parts full of water. None of us would have ever been seen again, for of those who once get into the Hooghly, few ever come out alive. As an example of how dangerous a place the James & Mary's are, I knew two fine iron ships which collided close to them. Both went on the quicksands, and in half an hour not a vestige of either was to be seen, and only two or three men of the crews were saved. The Comorin had fortunately gone on the only hard patch on the Sands.

While making a voyage to China in the ship Arracan, and while keeping a middle watch in the Indian Ocean, the night being calm and bright, and I leaning on the rail thinking of home and sweetheart, I was suddenly startled by a great light in the Heavens, and a rushing, hissing sound. Looking up I saw a ball of light coming, as it appeared, straight for us. Fortunately it fell in the water, not 100 feet from the ship, with a report like a cannon, and caused a swell which made the ship roll as in a heavy seaway. It was a big meteor and had it struck us it would have been "Good-bye Arracan." I am of the opinion that many vessels which have gone missing have been lost from this cause.

On one occasion I went with six of our apprentices in a boat to a small island in the China Sea, which had some large caves on it, and was surrounded by a

Coral reef. After picking up all the Coral we wanted, we decided to explore the island and caves, entering one of the latter in single file, I leading, and a lad named Boyes behind. We crept forward until the cave opened out into a dark and vaulted chamber, when suddenly we were startled by a great rushing, whirring sound, and young Boyes yelled out "Snakes". Instinctively one and all of us turned tail and made tracks for the outside. We studied not the order of our going, but 'got' and never stopped running until we reached the boat—a panic pure and simple. On reaching the boat I sat on the gunwale facing the cave, and what do you think I saw? Now, hold your breath reader, for it is what the ladies would call horrible, I saw a flock of great Bats coming out of the cave. They had been startled by us, and we, frightened by them. On seeing the cause of our fright, we just sat down and laughed until the tears ran down our cheeks. I never was in a real panic before or since, but my experience then taught me how easily they occur.

Another incident in which Master Boyes is concerned. A boat's crew and I had been exploring the River between Whampoo and Cantor, and it was dark on returning. Now in Whampoo Roads there was a large black buoy to mark the Western end of the anchorage, so I put Master Boyes on the lookout in the bow of the boat, telling him to keep a sharp look out for the buoy. Well, in about five minutes, crash went the boat into something, and young Boyes fell head over heels into the bottom of the boat, yelling at the top of his voice, "There it is Sir, there it is."

Of course the reader will quite understand that I

said a few gentle, but emphatic words, just to ease my feelings, and express my opinion of Master Boyes, for the boat's bow had been stove in, and I was bound to get a wigging from the shipper. Poor Boyes! After serving his time, he was made third mate of the ship Bombay and one dirty night while the crew were hauling aft the Jib sheet, he got on beforehand, and those behind, for reason unknown, let go, and he was whipped overboard and lost. The question at the time arose as to whether it had been done on purpose, for it only needed one man to ease up and the sheet would overpower the rest. I believe he was disliked by the men, which often happens from no apparent cause. I have experienced this myself, and very uncomfortable it is. Men will take an unaccountable dislike to a ship and officers, and nothing but a complete change both of officers and men will make things go smoothly.

I remember the first big fish I ever caught. It was a Bonito of about 15 lb weight. I was fishing from the jlb-boom, and when the fish in question took the hook, well, it seemed no trouble to pull it up, and then the struggle commenced. I held on like grim death, and yelled for all I was worth, but no-one heard me for a time. Finally, and just as help was coming, I had to let the fish go, or go overboard myself. You see I was sitting straddle-legs over a round spar, quite 60 feet from the ship. However, here goes for another fish story, which is perfectly true.

In ships of the Cormorin build, we had what was termed 'chains'. These were really wooden projections at right angles to ship's side, the same being spreaders for the rigging. Now in those days sailors were not provided with bath-rooms, and we used to go over the rail on to the spreader for a bath, taking a bucket and lanyard for drawing the water. Well, I was doing this one day and naturally wore the costume that Adam did before the fall. Standing with my back to the sea, and my face to the ship's side, I suddenly received a sounding smack on the part of my body that my mother used to play 'Rule Britannia' on with her slipper. I nearly fell overboard with the shock and just had time to see a big Flying Fish drop into the water. Now to this day I am not sure if that fish did it for a joke, or because it was shocked to see me in the costume in which I entered the World. Anyhow it is not everyone who has had his b-tt-m smacked by a Flying Fish.

At the time I was Chief Officer of the Ship Majestic, 1,900 tons register, under the Command of Captain W. Ellery, in the year 1878, we being homeward bound from Calcutta, with a few passengers on board, one of whom was a Doctor named Jones, a very eccentric man. He was in the habit of getting out of his bunk, reeking with perspiration, and coming to the dinner-table in his pants and singlet. This annoyed the Captain and other passengers, so the former asked me to speak to the Doctor quietly, and if possible get him to improve his manners—a thankless job for me in any case, but orders had to be obeyed. However, the Doctor was very indignant, and refused to alter his style of dinner-dress, and the skipper—who was a man of very little tact— undertook to administer a public rebuke, which he did as follows.

The Captain sitting at head of table, with the Doctor

on his left hand, and I next to the Doctor, the Captain audibly sniffing in the direction of Doctor Jones, looked towards me and said, "Don't you smell a sour disagreeable smell about here, Mr Goodwin?"

I replied, "Well, I do think there is a peculiar odour, Sir."

The Doctor gazed at me reproachfully, and then turned to the skipper with a look on his face which plainly said, "The Lord hath delivered thee into my hands, Oh mine enemy!"

"Captain," he quietly said. "Down in the little village where I was born, there was a half-witted man nicknamed Jimmy Smeller—on account of a habit he had of sniffing about and finding bad smells wherever he went. This was very annoying to the village folk, but at last they came to the conclusion that *it was Jimmy Smeller's own smell that Jimmy Smeller smelt.*"

What with the story and the disgusted look on the skipper's face at being smitten 'hip and thigh', the rest of us fairly exploded, for which I received a puerile rebuke after dinner, but then, as I said before, the Captain had but little tact, and I may add 'darned' little sense of humour.

I met Captain Ellery while home this last time (April 1908). He is now about 70 years old, and but for his hair being grey, he seemed very little different to what he was 30 years ago. He retired from sea about five years ago.

The following stories, although not properly connected with my life are, to some extent, characteristic of a type of Shipmaster that sailed the sea some 40 or 50 years ago and as a proof that the stories related are authentic,

144

I may say, I knew the ship and her Master, and also sailed, with her mate and some of her apprentices in another vessel, some forty to forty-two years ago.

The full-rigged ship Mindanao of about 400 tons register belonging to Messrs. T & J Brocklebank of Liverpool, was commanded by Captain John H. Ponsonby who, I may say was one of the most eccentric pompous and autocratic old gentlemen that ever sailed the salt seas as Master in the Cape Horn trade, and when he fitted himself up to the bung-hole with good Jamaica rum he was dangerous, owing to his habit of fooling with fire-arms when in that condition.

The mate's name was John A. Leach, a fine seaman, but an indifferent officer, and Captain Ponsonby held him in great contempt. On more than one occasion something like this would happen. Captain P. would come on deck in the middle morning watch, and the latter would say, "Morning Sir; heavy dew falling during the night. I wonder what is the cause of it?"

"The cause of it, Sir," Captain Ponsonby would reply, "is the voice of Nature telling you to set those Royals. How dare you delay my ship for want of canvas. Go to your room, Sir, at once," and John would go—nothing loath—for he knew he was in for a good twelve hours rest.

When he had got safely into his bunk, the skipper would go down into the cabin and call out, "Steward, bring my seal and some sealing-wax," and would then proceed to seal up the mate's door, which he would keep sealed until evening. He would then knock at the door and call out, "Are you there Mr Leach?"

"Yes, I am here Sir."

"Oh you are, are you!—would you like a glass of grog, Sir?" And John would smack his lips and say, "Thank you Captain," for he was getting jolly well empty having no food all day. Capt. P. would remain silent for a few minutes, and then say, "So you would like a drop of grog, would you?"

"Yes, Sir," the mate would answer.

"I'll see you damned first," would be the startling reply. "Come out of your room and go to your duty at once, Sir."

On one occasion when lying in Callao, Captain P. considered he had been insulted by the Manager of a Ship Chandler's Store, and he determined to get even with him. So he called at the Store one Saturday, and made himself very agreeable to the Manager, who thought that Captain P. had quite forgotten their little difference—but he did not know his man, as the sequel will show. However, Captain P. said to him, "Oh, by-the-bye, Mr So-and-So, tomorrow being Sunday, perhaps you would come off to my ship for dinner, and bring your wife with you." This the Manager did, arriving on board early in the forenoon.

Now Captain P. was an adept at single-sticks [martial art, used in training] of which fact the poor Manager was not aware, so when Captain P. said, "By-the-Bye, Mr ----- , the dinner won't be ready for an hour or so, so what do you say to a bout at single-sticks, it will pass the time, and give us an appetite for dinner." So what could the poor Manager do but acquiesce, at the same time declaring he did not know much about the game. Well, to cut the story short, in a few minutes Capt. P. had the man crying out for mercy, and his wife begging the mate to interfere, which he would not do, saying it was no business of his. So after Captain P. had satisfied his wounded vanity, he desisted, and said, "There, Sir, that will teach you to insult Captain Ponsonby. Mr Leach, put the jolly-boat over the side, and send two of the dirtiest boys in the ship to pull these people ashore."

After this, Captain P. used to go on shore with a cutlass by his side, and a revolver in his pocket. He knew he had gone too far, and Callao was a wild place in those days.

The Mindanao was a flush-decked ship and had two cabins down below, the fore one for the officers, and the after one for the Master, and as it was in the latter that the following incident occurred, I will give a rough description of it, to help the reader understand what may be called the 'Stage Setting'.

Across the stern of a wooden vessel run heavy transverse timbers called Transomes. These, in this ship were cased in by teak-wood panels, and a semi-circular seat made round the stern, in the centre of which were two arms forming a seat of honour for the Captain, with sitting room for three persons on each side of him.

Filling in the circle was placed a wooden table with a drawer in it opposite the Captain's seat in which Captain P. always kept two loaded revolvers, and on the bulkhead opposite the Captain was a large mirror. The door leading to the companion exit was on the port corner, and the cabin was always lighted on state occasions by candles in big silver candle-sticks, one each side of the Captain.

The 'Dramatis Personae' on this occasion were:

Captain P.

Four visiting Captains

Ship's steward, and a sailor (the latter a clever broken-down University man)

Port – Iquique [Chile]

Time – 8 p.m.

Now Captain P. considered himself a fine scholar, and was given to quoting Latin and Greek words, and during the course of conversation he quoted a certain Greek word to emphasize some statement he had made. The meaning of this word was at once disputed by one of the visitors, and Captain P. in his bumptious manner said, "I will soon prove to you that I am right, Sir—Steward, tell John So-and-So to come aft," which he did, the man appearing at the cabin door in his bare feet, pants rolled up, and shirt-neck open—the 'Beau Ideal' of a tarry sailor, and then the following dialogue ensued.

Captain P. "Now, John—is not the meaning of such and such a Greek word, so and so?"

Sailor. "Yes, Sir, that is quite correct."

Captain P. "Thank you. Now go to the steward and he will give you a glass of grog," and then turning to his friends said, "I told you I was right, Gentlemen."

Chorus of visitors. "We object, and are not accustomed to sailors being brought aft to settle Cabin arguments, and consider we have been insulted by your doing so."

Captain P. "Oh, you do! Well, I want you to understand

that any man whom I consider good enough for my cabin is good enough for you or anyone else," and swiftly pulling out the drawer and blowing the candles out, he commenced firing both revolvers indiscriminately round the cabin.

A pandemonium then ensued that beggars description —men on their hands and knees shouting and cursing. Bang, bang! went the guns, smash! went the mirror, and when the revolvers were exhausted, in rushed the officers and crew, secured old Ponsonby, locked him in his room, hustled the visitors into a boat, and pulled them away to their several ships, they in the meantime vowing vengeance on Captain P. and all his family, unto the third and fourth generation.

Now, the primary cause of all this turmoil, dear reader, was good old Jamaica Rum, but just one more yarn!

Ship Mindanao close hauled on the starboard tack, heading up for the Straits of Le Mare, an apprentice at the wheel (afterwards a shipmate of mine and from whose lips I heard this yarn), wind begins to head the ship off. Captain P. walking the weather side, alternately looking up at the sails and squinting into the Compass. Ship suddenly breaks off two Points.

"Damn you, Sir," the skipper passionately said, "you are bringing me a head wind—you Jonah you. Steward," he bawled down the companionway, "bring me my gun." The gun was brought, and while Captain P. was coolly loading it, my friend was shaking in his shoes, not knowing what was going to happen. Having loaded the gun, the skipper walked to the mizzen-mast, went down on one knee, and coolly took aim at the helmsman, and after covering him for some time, he slowly raised the gun and fired over his head. Then walking aft he said, "Do you think Captain Ponsonby would hurt a hair of your head? No! my boy, not on any account—keep your luff boy—luff and touch her."

The latter order sharply given restored my friend's nerves to their normal condition, for as he afterwards put it, "I was having a rotten bad attack of the shakes."

I have no doubt the reader will say, "Has this man never been brought to book for these little eccentricities?"

Well, he was once fined one hundred dollars for putting a gendarme off his horse, taking his sword from him and then giving him a good thrashing. That was the only known occasion when Justice overtook him. And as far as I know, he died with his boots off, which is more than many a man has done who was fond of making a display with firearms. "Verily the wicked man spreadeth himself like a green Bay tree."

With the latter remark, I will conclude the Chronicles of Captain Ponsonby, and will give two Toasts which were very common in sailor town in my young days, just to prevent them being lost to the world now that the sailor-man is passing away.

### FAIR LADIES TOAST

*Here's to the tar, I smell it far,*
*It is sweeter than the Rose,*
*And here's to the boy that's far away,*
*That wears the tarry clothes.*

# TARRY SAILORS

*From rocks and sands and barren lands*
*May I protected be,*
*From great guns and women's tongues*
*The Lord deliver me.*

Not very gallant, but tarry John paid the shot, and as long as he had one in his locker, why, he said what he pleased, and it was only when the locker was empty that his so-called friends said, "Rise up Jack and let John sit down, for you see he is 'Homeward Bound'."

On conclusion of the 'Ponsonby' Chronicles, I fully intended to cease spinning any more yarns, firstly, because I was not satisfied with what I had already written, and secondly, because I had an indolent fit on, due perhaps to the hot weather, but the clouds having rolled away, I have taken up a new thread, and sat the spinning-jenny to work once more, twisting up another yarn.

Somewhere about the year 1897, I had as passenger from Liverpool to Singapore, a gentleman named Houghton, who was on his way to Sumatra for big game shooting. He and I became very friendly, he told me many stories of his past life. He had for a few years owned a big Cattle Ranch in one of the Western States of America, and taken a very active part in putting down cattle-stealing. Indeed he had been a very prominent member of a vigilante committee. So well was he hated by the crowd who live on the border-land between respectability and crime, that his death had been determined upon.

On several occasions he was shot at, and so great was their hatred towards him, that he could never stir out unless accompanied by two of his Cow-boys with fingers on trigger, ready to shoot on sight in defence of their employer. Mr Houghton stood this for 12 months, until he found that the strain began to tell on him, so gathering his men together, one evening, he and they made a dash across country (100 miles) to the Railway, where he took the train Eastwards, leaving his head man in charge of the Ranch.

On arrival in Chicago he entered into negotiations for the sale of his ranch and when this business was arranged he came home to England.

Now one of the stories he related to me was about a rain-making incident, which is so extraordinary that it is difficult to believe it, but Mr Houghton gave me his word of honour as an English gentleman that the story was true, and that he himself was a prominent factor in the case.

The town of Cheyenne in one of the Western States of America was a great centre for Cattle ranchers, who when tired of the solitude of the plains, met there to discuss business and drinks.

Now Cheyenne is a very dry place, and is situated in a deep valley between high mountains, the ground sloping away from the hills at one end, right down to the Great Plains at the other end, and up to the time when my story begins, no rain was ever known to fall in the Valley. So one day when a typical tenderfoot, with a couple of carpet-bags, arrived in the town and after asking for, and seeing the Mayor, offered for the sum of One Thousand Dollars to bring rain within three weeks, provided his conditions were complied with. One can imagine the amazement of the Mayor, who was quite justified in thinking he had a crank to deal with, but being a bit of a sport, and the boys (cattle-ranchers) also being in great force at the time, he went round to the Hotel and placed the proposition before them, and they being quite prepared to do anything which would promise a little excitement, promptly took the matter up, subscribed the money and elected a Committee to see the matter through—Mr Houghton being elected Chairman.

On the rain-maker being interviewed, he named as his conditions that a hut should be lent him, just outside the town, and that a circle of two hundred yards around it should be staked off, and that guards should be stationed day and night to keep people off, that food should be placed daily in the hands of one of the guards, from whom he would take it, but no-one was to come inside the circle on any pretence until the three weeks had expired or until rain had fallen. In the latter case he was to get 1,000 Dollars, and be escorted to, and placed on board the train for the West, or if no rain came he was to be dealt with in any manner the Committee might decide.

Now, this was a fair sporting offer and the boys were delighted with the prospect of having some fun. So matters were arranged at once and the next day the rain-maker carrying two carpet-bags—which he refused to allow anyone to touch—was escorted to the hut.

Guards were placed, and the crowd were warned that anyone going inside the circle would be shot at sight. The next morning a small tube was seen projecting above the roof of the shanty, but the rain-maker was not visible. Day after day passed away, the man taking his food regularly, but speaking to no-one. Soon nearly every man in the place had bets on, and when the Eighteenth day came, and no signs of rain, the baser sort began to be restless, and threats were made of forcing the circle and lynching the tenderfoot, who they said was playing them for suckers (the latter word is an Americanism). So the committee turned out their friends and the place was so well guarded, that even a rabbit could not have got through. Mr Houghton told me he had been very much impressed with the man's earnestness, and although he himself was sceptical, he was fully determined the man should have his full scope of rope even to the bitter end.

However, to be brief, the morning of the twentieth day was as usual, bright and clear, but at noon, clouds began to gather over the head hills, and grew heavier and heavier as the hours passed on. The excitement in the town was intense, for clouds had never before been seen over the hills. At five o'clock the thunder was rolling and the lightning became very vivid, and at 6 p.m. it was raining a perfect deluge—the main street was practically a torrent, and the water rushing down it into the Plains destroyed acres of farm land, indeed doing some thousands of dollars worth of damage,

When the storm was over, the farmers from the Plains came into the valley with the expressed intention of lynching the man who had brought a deluge instead of gentle rain. The Committee however got the man safely away, and then the farmers turned on the Chairman and demanded compensation. This being refused, they brought an Action in the Law Court to recover damages.

They were not successful with their claim, but they certainly gave the Committee a great deal of trouble.

Now, I have no doubt but that my readers will ask if I believe this story. Well, I do believe the man offered to make the rain, and that the other facts of the story are true, but whether the man had the power he professed to have, or whether it was really a lucky co-incidence, I must let the reader judge for themselves, but I will remind those who doubt, 'That Truth is stranger than Fiction'.

I will now, in sailor language conclude my yarns, clap a stopper on my jaw tackle and belay full due, for:

*To sail the seas is my delight,*
*And bend a bowline on a bight,*
*To fish the crossjack yard and haul*
*On topsail lifts true bliss I call.*
*I climb the giddy fullock shrouds,*
*And fling my navolines to the crowd.*
*With a Ye-ho!—Heave ho!—Ye ho!*

*And so till cruel fate forbids,*
*I'll dwell mid marline spikes and Fids,*
*And dissipate all thoughts of gloom,*
*With a Bobstay or a stunsail boom.*
*If life with sorrows crowns my cup,*
*I'll send my Mizzen Topsail up,*
*And with a sneer the chafing gear,*
*I calmly bid it disappear.*

# Chapter 15

*1908 Second Steward lost—Capt. Devenish taken ill—song from Dreadnought days—a plea for good pensions for sailors*

I arrived—as before stated—in Liverpool, on the 1st of October 1908, and had a very pleasant time at home, being relieved from all duty, until the ship was again ready for sea.

I saw my son while at home, his ship the Orestes arriving soon after I did. I may add that just before he got home, his wife presented him with another son, who has been named Sydney, this being the first time the name has been used in our branch of the Goodwins. In this instance, the child is named after his Mother's brother.

The weather during my stay at home was exceedingly good, but too warm for the time of the year. Nevertheless, it suited me, and lasted out my stay home, but I fear those at home will have to suffer later on for the abnormal heat, and I am looking forward to hearing that they are having a cold hard winter.

Going back to the period before my arrival home, I may say that my home-coming was more anxiously looked for than usual, the reason being that on the 30th of September 1898, my wife's sister Jessie, and her husband, William Parry, were to celebrate their Golden Wedding, and they greatly desired my presence, but unfortunately I did not arrive until the day after the celebrations—this was a great disappointment to us all. I think this is as an appropriate time as any to say a few words about William Parry and my family. He was for some years the special Liverpool Pilot for the Pacific Steam Navigation Co, and he left them about the year 1876 to become Master of the Huskisson Dock. From there he went to the Lungton and Alexandra Docks, on their being opened. He afterwards became Assistant Harbour Master, from which post he retired on pension in the year 1902. I may mention that the above William and Jessie Parry have had six children—three sons and three daughters. James, the eldest son, was lost in the ship Bay Of Biscay, which disappeared with all hands in the Bay of Biscay in the year 1879. Richard is, at the present time, Dock-Master of the Alfred Dock, Birkenhead.

The third son, Tom, who was also a sailor, died at Bootle in 1906, and was buried in Anfield Cemetery. The daughters are, Minnie, unmarried, Margaret, who is married to William Isaacs (Issue—one son named Stanley), and Jessie, married to D. MacNicol, who died in the year 1903, leaving his wife and one daughter, Elaine, to mourn for him.

I have given these few particulars, because I often asked my elders, and others in turn have asked me, "Who is so and so?" Perhaps referring to a second cousin, with an unfamiliar name.

We sailed from Liverpool on the 31st of October on the usual voyage to Straits, China, and Japan. The morning after leaving we unfortunately lost our second steward, he having gone missing. There is no way of accounting for his disappearance, except by suicide, it being absolutely impossible for him to have fallen overboard. No-one saw or heard him go, nor did we credit he had gone, but thought he had hid himself. I have seen that done on many occasions, having lost men for five to 12 hours, drink, sleepyhead, illness, or an unaccountable impulse to hide himself have been the causes, and it is wonderful how a man can hide on board a ship when he gives his mind to it. I have seen all hands with half a dozen policemen search a ship for Stowaways without finding anyone, and then five or six turn up 24 hours after we had sailed.

We arrived at Penang and Singapore in due course, and sailed from the latter port on the 5th of December 1908, for Shanghai. As this is a bad season for getting up the China Sea, owing to strong N.E. Monsoons, and contrary currents, I determined to take the route East of Formosa, and thus get into the Japan Current. This we accomplished and had a fine run up close along the Island for 200 miles, with lovely warm weather, and dark blue seas. There is a sudden change after opening out the North end of the Island, when the weather becomes colder, and the water changes to an Olive Green. This means that we are leaving the warm Stream flowing N.E. and are getting into the Arctic current, which flows down the coast of China to the South-West. The change of temperature is very sudden, and some people feel it very much, and I now-a-days have to be careful to get into warm clothes quickly, for should I get a chill, my old enemy—Malaria Fever—gives me a turn, and it is "no pleasant, ye ken," as the Scotchman says.

We arrived at Shanghai on the 14th of December, and after a stay of three days we proceeded to Nagasaki, and Moji. At the latter place, my friend, Captain Devenish, boarded us to pilot us through the inland Sea. I thought he did not look at all well, and I regret to say that when about forty miles from Kobe, he lost all sense of direction, or where he was going, and I had to send him below, and take the ship on myself. On talking to Devenish after arrival, I found him quite clear in his mind, on all subjects, except with regard to what had happened, and he considered I must have been a little off my head in taking the ship out of his hands. He held this view, notwithstanding the fact that he had actually turned the ship round and was going back to Moji a few minutes before I went on deck and found he had done so. Of course I had to report the matter to my Agents, advising a long holiday, as I did not consider him to be in a fit condition to take charge of a ship. The foregoing occurrence placed me in an exceedingly unpleasant position. First, I had to report my friend, and then break the news to his wife. We spent our Christmas in Kobe, but it was not a merry one for me, owing to my being so upset over Devenish.

We sailed from Yokohama on the 5th of January 1909 for Kobe, and on arrival there, heard that my friend Captain Devenish was in the Hospital at Yokohama, he having gone to the latter place for a change, but broke down and was ordered by the Doctor into Hospital for treatment, which I trust will be effective. From Kobe we went to Shanghai, Hong-Kong, and Singapore, picking up cargo at the various ports for Genoa, Marseilles, and Liverpool.

We have been hearing a great deal lately of the decadence of British seamen, and while there is some truth in what is said, there is also a good deal of nonsense spoken. The sailor has simply had to change with the change from wood to iron ships, and from sail to steam. I can fairly claim to be a sailor of the 'old school', having been brought up in wooden ships—rope rigging, single topsails, studding sails, fine marline-spike work, hand pumps and fleet over windlass—the latter a straight barrelled affair, with two turns of the cable around it, and as we hove up the anchor, the chain travelled from one side of the barrel to the other. When it was close over, the order was, "Fleet over, clap on the devil's claw on the fore part, and then slack up the turns and shift them to the other side".

Now all this went to the making of a good seaman of the time, but it has now passed away, just as much as a great many details in the rigging and build of a ship had almost passed away before my time. The noble line of battleship, the Dutch galliot, and the North Sea Collier brig, the then grand training ground and vessels for sailors—all passed away in the first ten years of my sea life, followed quickly by the 'Tea Clippers' and the grand vessels in the Australian and New York passenger trade. Of the latter, the Dreadnought, there was a song which used to be sung in ships' forecastles when I was a boy. I give the few verses I remember of it below.

*There's a saucy bold Packet, a Packet of Fame,*
*She hails from New York*
*and the Dreadnought's her name,*
*She sails to the Westward*

*where the strong winds do blow,*
*She's a Liverpool packet—brave boys let her go.*

*Now she is lying in the River Mersey,*
*Waiting for the Constitution*
*to tow us away.*
*We gave three loud cheers*
*while the TEARS down flow.*
*She's a Liverpool packet—brave boys let her go.*

*Now we are sailing on the ocean so wide,*
*And the deep and blue waters*
*dash against our black side,*
*Our sail set so neatly*
*and the black ball flag shew,*
*She's a Liverpool packet—brave boys let her go.*

*And now we are sailing along the Long Island shore*
*When the Pilot, he boards,*
*as he's oft' done before,*
*Saying, "Fill your main topsail*
*your fore Jack also,*
*She's a Liverpool packet—brave boys let her go."*

The Constitution was a noted Liverpool Tug in the early sixties (1860). Her sisters were, The United States, and Brother Jonathon. They were all powerful paddle-tugs, and did much in their day to make and retain the reputation of the Liverpool Tugs, which were the best in the world at that time.

TEARS—the Dreadnought carried Irish Emigrants to New York, and the scenes witnessed beggar description—

both tears and hair fell, and 'Celtic Nature' gave full scope to its capacity for weeping and wailing.

I myself witnessed one scene in Queenstown Harbour that I shall never forget. As the ship left the pier, some of the women relations of the passengers threw themselves on the ground, and clawed and bit the earth—others tried to throw themselves into the water, and all were wailing like Banshees.

More changes are still going on, many of which we older sailors do not approve, but we have to submit and unlearn much that we knew, and adapt ourselves to the new order of things. Nevertheless, I claim that every officer and seaman would be the better of training under sail. It makes a more resourceful man of him, a thing which is needed on board of a ship—be she a sailing vessel or steamer.

The great question is, who is to provide the sailing ships, and find work for them? It is said that English boys don't want to go to sea now-a-days, because all the romance is knocked out of it, and I believe it is quite true, but I also believe that the rising generation think it beneath their dignity to do the hard work necessary on board a ship, too much education of the wrong sort, a dislike to discipline, and too much cuffs and collars is at the bottom of it all. Nevertheless the sailor of the day is still with us, and just as ready to go into the lifeboat to save life, and to let the women and children go first into safety, as ever his predecessor was.

Before closing, I will say, that long ago the people of England should have seen that all seamen and officers should have a pension, say at 55 or 60 years of age—funds to be collected on the contributor basis, all unclaimed seamen's wages, and a proportion of the Light Dues should go into the fund. Some day the time will come they will get it, that is, when the Nation realises that the seaman ranks next to the Agriculturalist in the Political economy of the nation.

We arrived at Suez on the morning of February 19th 1909, having experienced a heavy sand-storm coming up the Gulf of Suez, which gave me a very anxious time navigating. Fog is bad, but a sand-storm is worse. However, we arrived all right, and in due time passed through the Canal, and left Port Said for Genoa, arriving there on the 26th February in a snowstorm.

We left in due course for Marseilles, arriving there March 1st, the weather being the coldest I have ever experienced in the Mediterranean. It was my intention to have come through the Straits of Messina [between Sicily and Italy] and there have seen the effects of the terrible Earthquake, but I received orders not to go through owing to feared changes in the Coast-line.

We left Marseilles at 7 a.m. on the 2nd March, and after a stormy passage arrived at Liverpool on the 10th of March, and found all well.

# Chapter 16

I arrived home on the 10th March, and found all fairly
well, with the exception of my wife's sister, who, I regret
to say, was slowly passing away to the 'Great Beyond',
and to our sorrow and her gain, she entered into rest on
the 19th March 1909. My wife was with her sister at the
last, but the latter was quite unconscious, and passed
quietly and painlessly away at 9 p.m. She was 74 years
of age, and was buried at Anfield Cemetery, in the same
grave as her son Tom. The day after her sister's death,
my wife had an attack of Influenza, which kept her to
her bed and room for ten days. Then I took it, and had
it off and on—attended by Malaria—until I sailed again.
Some four weeks before I arrived home, Carrie, my eldest
daughter had an attack, and entirely lost her voice for
some three weeks, recovering it all at once after I had
been home about five days.

During the time I was away, my sister, Mrs Eleanor
Bagnal, removed to Liverpool from Belfast, her son
Charles having completed his apprenticeship at Messrs.
Workman & Clark's shipbuilding yard. He joined the
Nelson Line of steamers as an engineer, and went to
Buenos Aires on his first voyage.

I had letters from my cousins, Bessie Cargill, née
Goodwin, also my cousin J. M. Goodwin, of Melbourne,

and my friend Captain Lowry of Newcastle, County Down, Ireland—all were well when they wrote. On the 8th of April, I went up to Glasgow to bring my ship to Liverpool, but had to go to bed on arrival at Glasgow, with a heavy cold and Malaria Fever, only getting up at noon on the 10th to take charge of the ship. I did not feel fit, but it was my own fault I was there.

Gladys Goodwin, my brother Edward's daughter—now a certified Nurse and Midwife—came to see me while in Glasgow. She is a fine big woman, and will I hope do well in her profession.

Jack, my son, arrived in London on the 15th April, from Australia, and would sail thence for Liverpool on the 18th April, I sailing on the same day for China and Korea. My Grandsons—Jack's children—are growing up fine little fellows, and I trust they will become as good in life at they are in looks.

We called at Jeddah on the passage for a few Pilgrims, taking some to Singapore. From the latter port, we went on to Hong Kong, Shanghai, and Taku Bar. From thence we went to Dalny—the terminus of the South Manchurian Railway, and the spoils of war to the Japanese from the Russians. I found it a town in course of construction, and could not help admiring the energy displayed by the Japanese in trying to make the Railway and Town a commercial and financial success.

I spent my 59th birthday in Dalny, and left the following day, June 9th, for Chemulpo, in Korea. Chemulpo is rather a difficult port for a stranger to get to, but we arrived and left there in safety. This was my first visit to Korea, and I must say I was favourably impressed with the climate and people, though I saw both at their very best. From Chemulpo, we sailed for Kuchinotou, Japan, to fill our coal bunkers, arriving there on the 14th June, and sailing again on the 15th for Makasser and Sourabaya [both Indonesia] and I suppose other ports on the Coast of Java.

My letters from home have so far been very satisfactory, and I hear my son is still in the S.S. Orestes and will be in Hong Kong about the 20th June, so I shall miss him this voyage.

We left Kuchinotou on the 15th June, and arrived at Makassar on the 23rd of the same month. I found the latter place rather interesting, and enjoyed my visit very much. We sailed on the 26th for a place called Kraksaan, in Java, and from there we went to Sourabaya, at which place we remained for ten days, sailing on the 10th July for Pasoeroean and Samarang, and after a stay at the latter Port of three days, we went to Cheribon for Pilgrims, and thence to Batavia to complete our loading and take on some more Pilgrims for Jeddah. The weather from leaving Kuchinotou until arrival at Batavia was very rainy indeed, quite unseasonable, this being the dry season on the Java Coast, and a great deal of damage has been done to the Sugar Crops. Nevertheless we are walking off with some 4,400 tons, the balance of our cargo being Tea, Coffee, Spices, Tapioca, Flour, Rubber, and various other articles of Produce.

We left Batavia on the 19th July, taking the route North of the Chagoos Archipelago and Seychelle Islands, the principal Island of the latter group, Mahe, being located as the site of the Garden of Eden by the late General

Gordon, he saying that on the Island grows a tree which bears two kinds of Fruit, this tree growing nowhere else in the World. Of course he gave other reasons for his theory, but it is not my province to enter into details, only mentioning the matter as being of local interest and colouring.

We had some difficulty in making the land round Ras Hajoun [eastern tip of Somalia] and Cape Guaudifui, owing to thick weather, and arriving there at night. After getting round the latter Cape we had hot sultry weather, the atmosphere being full of fine dust which parched one's throat.

My firemen who had suffered more or less from Malaria Fever, were unable to stand the intense heat, and went off duty one by one from heat exhaustion.

My Chief Engineer in describing the heat said, "Coming out of the stokehole on deck, was like coming out of Hell into a Blast-furnace"—very forcible, but an apt illustration.

We sailed into Perim for a small supply of Coal, and then proceeded to Jeddah, to land our Pilgrims, then on to Suez, at which port we heard that our ship was to load outwards for Australia on our next voyage. After passing through the Canal, we cooled and got our letters from 'Home Sweet Home', and sailed on the 12th August for Amsterdam. I may mention that our firemen all seem to have recovered their usual health, so I hope we shall have no trouble in that respect.

We arrived at Amsterdam on the 25th August, sailed for London on the 27th, arriving there on the 28th, and after doing my ship's inwards business, I got down home the same evening, and was thankful to find my dear wife and daughters all well, with the exception of Bessie, who I regret to say is anything but strong, having I fear been fretting and worrying a good deal. The Goodwins worry a good deal over very little, and she is no exception to the rule.

I joined my ship in London on the 2nd September, and left for Liverpool on the 3rd, docking at Queen's Dock, Liverpool, on 5th September. My steamer left Liverpool for Glasgow on the 5th September, in charge of the Chief Officer, Mr Bebb. I am to join her about the 30th September, and sail on the 2nd October 1909 for Australia.

# Chapter 17

*1909 To Australia again—meeting the family*

After a pleasant stay at home (marred somewhat by my daughter Bessie being ill—though I am thankful to say she was recovering her strength when I left home) the time again came when I had once more to turn my back on those dear to me, and set out on a long sea journey. However, just before I sailed, my son Jack came home, and we had the pleasure of meeting now and again. This coming voyage he goes to Japan, and I to Australia. I am glad to go there, for I am looking forward to seeing my cousins John M. Goodwin, and Ella Robinson.

We sailed from Glasgow on the 2nd October 1909, and passed the Cape of Good Hope on the 24th, 22 days 4 hours from Glasgow. I expected to have done it in less time, but the S.E. trades were strong, and against us. We experienced strong Westerly gales, and very cool weather running our Easting down and arrived in Port Adelaide on the 14th November, passage 42 days 14 hours. I found it much the same as I left it eight years ago. Of course there are improvements in the approaches, and in the town itself, but nothing startling, nevertheless I found some old friends, and it seemed just like as if I had never been away from the place.

After a stay in Adelaide of five days, we went on to Melbourne, arriving there on the 21st in a regular N.N.W.

buster, or gale. We were in rather a critical situation in the River, and I was thankful to get the steamer fast to the wharf. The dust that was flying about Melbourne on that good Sunday—21st November 1909—was something awful.

My cousin, Jack Goodwin, met me the day after arrival. I found him looking very frail and old, but the same good fellow he always was. I also saw Ella Robinson, and my Uncle Sam Taylor, who is 88 years of age, and I met his daughter Nellie Taylor, who I had not seen for years—not since 1862 in Dublin, 45 years ago, nearly half a century. Of course I did not know her, but she is a lady in every sense of the term, and a most dutiful daughter—so different from the usual Australians, who as far as I can see usually disrespect their parents.

From Melbourne I went to Sydney, and there met my sister Annie, her husband (A. Maxwell) and their eldest daughter Ellie (Mrs Singleton), who has had a short and sad experience of married life, being separated from her husband, who turned out utterly worthless, and absolutely failed to provide for her. No-one knows where he is now, and Ellie does not want to know, and refuses to be called Mrs Singleton. She is now known as Miss Maxwell. It is a great blessing there were no children by the marriage. Flossie Maxwell—who is a Hospital Nurse at Newcastle, N.S.W.—came down to see me. She is a fine young woman, but inclined to flirt. Ernie Maxwell is married, and is somewhere in the Bush—about 200 miles from Sydney.

I may mention that a coal strike was declared when

I arrived at Adelaide, and although hopes of settlement were entertained, the strike continues, and was going on when I left Adelaide homewards on the 4th February 1910. Of course the strike seriously affected all steamships, and detained us some weeks longer in Australia than we otherwise should have been.

I left Sydney December 3rd, and arrived at Brisbane on the 5th, and found the town much larger than when I first saw it, and also renewed my acquaintance with a few people I might call friends. At Brisbane we came to a full stop for want of Coal, but after sundry interviews with Coal people, and the man's representatives, we managed to secure 1,400 tons. We got the Coal very slowly, as we only got the surplus over the daily local requirements. The Queensland miners were not on strike, but would only supply those who were old customers, thus helping the Southern miners by not supplying outside ships.

After spending a pleasant time, with beautiful weather until two days before Christmas, the weather then broke, and it rained in torrents for four days, Xmas Day being an exceptionally wet day. Nevertheless I went out to dinner to our Agent's house (Mr Bleachmore), and spent a very pleasant day with him and his good lady.

On the 31st of December, I received orders to sail the next day for Hobart, Tasmania, which I did, sailing on New Year's Day 1910, and arriving at Hobart on the morning of the 5th January. I found Hobart a very enjoyable place, and probably the easiest going place in the Australian Commonwealth. We remained there 17 days, so I had an opportunity of judging. Nevertheless I liked the place very much indeed, and enjoyed my visit.

From Hobart we proceeded to Melbourne, and after a stay of six days—during which time I saw all my cousins, also my wife's relations—I left there. Of course one is always rushed in the places you would like most time, but I spent a pleasant time on the whole. My wife's two cousins Harriet and Margaret Rae, left Melbourne on the 1st of February 1910, on a visit to England. I left on the 29th January, but my stay in Adelaide covered their arrival and departure on the mail boat at the latter port, so I spent the best part of the day with them. They sailed for Colombo on the 3rd February by mail steamer, and I left the next morning for the same port. I arrived on the 20th and sailed the same day for Suez, arriving there on the 4th of March, and after passing through the Canal, we left Port Said on the 5th for Dunkirk, where we arrived on the 16th, after a moderate passage. On the 20th March we sailed for London, and docked on 21st March, thus completing a voyage of 5 months and 22 days.

# Chapter 18

*1910 A survivor found—King Edward dies—meets the Devenishes in Kobe—14 deaths among pilgrims on board*

On the 16th April 1910, I sailed for the Straits of Malacca, Hong Kong, Takao in Formosa, and to various ports in Japan.

We made a fair and uninteresting passage until the 7th May, when we picked up a boat belonging to the Seychelle Islands, which had on board one dead, and one living skeleton. They had been adrift for four months, sailing aimlessly about, lost on the wide wide sea. The survivor told me he had subsisted on raw fish which they caught, and had been drinking salt water for quite a month before we found them. Previous to that they caught rain-water from time to time. It appears the skipper of the boat took a lot of Rum with him, and never stopped drinking until it was finished, and as he persisted in steering the first night out, I presume he saw two compasses or snakes, or something like that, and so lost the Island and himself. The weather being misty the next day, nothing was to be seen. However, I annex a statement made by the Survivor, in which, by my advice, he suppressed the Rum part of the business, because it is always best to "let sleeping dogs lie" when possible, and the man paid for his spree with his life— indeed it was his body that was found in the boat [*See 'A Survivor Found At Sea' on page 265*].

On the night of the 12th May, the P. & O. steamer Palma signalled to us that King Edward was dead. We were all much grieved, and I personally think we have lost one of the finest Kings that ever sat on a Throne. May God comfort his Queen and family. Personally, I am a Royalist to the tips of my finger ends, and look on Democracy with a good deal of contempt, as I notice in all Parliaments, Councils, and Senates, the strong Member always rules the rest. There is no getting away from the good old rule, the simple plan, that he shall take who has the power, and he shall keep who can. May God bless King George the Fifth, and grant him a long, happy and successful reign.

We arrived at Penang and Singapore in due course, and at the latter place landed our castaway, and shipped 750 Chinese passengers for Hong Kong. The first day out, one jumped overboard, and was drowned, the next day another went mad, and one started to steal, so I had to put them both in Irons—to save one from himself, and the other from the vengeance of those he tried to rob.

We arrived at Hong Kong on the evening of the 22nd, and sailed again on the morning of the 24th, for a place called Takao, in the Island of Formosa. We lie there in an open Roadstead, and it takes very little wind to stop our work, and as we have 5,000 tons of machinery to put out, we have a big job on hand, and I fear a long one. Contrary to my expectations, we did excellent work at Takao, getting away in 11 days, only three of which we did no work owing to bad weather.

We left Takao on the 6th June, and after calling at

Kuchinotsu, Nagasaki, Moji, and Kobe, we arrived at Yokohama on the 14th June, and left again for Sourabaya, in the Island of Java on the morning of the 19th. While in Kobe, I saw my friends—the Devenishes—and regret to say that Captain Devenish has not recovered his mind, and I fear he never will. His wife is having a hard time of it, and from my heart I pity her, and trust she will have strength to bear the burden placed upon her.

I hear there is much controversy over the King's Oath to uphold the Protestant Religion. Now, while admitting that at first sight it is hard on Roman Catholics to hear the essential points of their Religion—the class and worship of the Virgin—called superstitious, yet we Protestants believe that the worship and belief in such doctrines are both idolatrous and superstitious, and the Oath was made strong to protect us from attempts being made by King, Clergy, Peers or Commons, to force this belief on us.

I can trust a lay Catholic (English), but no Priest or Brotherhood that was ever created. We are the top dog just now, and we shall be fools if we give up our position. Nevertheless, we are going to do it, or at least the Political Nonconformist peace-at-any-price Government are. This is not a prophesy, but simply reading the signs of the times. Oh! What fools we English are, and when shall we cease to be so. But I am forgetting that I am not writing a political treatise, but a few of the incidents of my life, so will now return to that subject.

We arrived at Sourabaya on the 29th June 1910, and there told that we were to take over 1,000 pilgrims to Jeddah, in addition to cargo for Amsterdam and

Liverpool—a nice prospect, seeing that Cholera was very bad in Java, and we had to, and did go, to eleven ports in Java, collecting the Pilgrims, but by God's mercy, we were spared from infection. It was a great worry and anxiety to me, as we went from port to port, dreading that at the next port I might get the disease on board. However, we finally arrived at Batavia with 600 people on board, and after a three days stay, we left for Padang, in the Island of Sumatra, with 1,136 pilgrims and 79 crew, or 1,212 persons on board.

At Padang we landed all the Pilgrims, who were medically inspected and vaccinated, and re-shipped— the latter business was only a dodge to get a clean Bill of Health for Kamaran, where the pilgrims will be landed and undergo ten days Quarantine. The ship in the meantime will be disinfected and cleaned, then the Pilgrims will re-embark, and we will proceed to Jeddah and land them, and there is not a man on board but will thank God from the bottom of his heart when we see the last of them.

The Pilgrim trade is 'rotten'—as my son Jack calls it—who by the way I had the pleasure of seeing while in Sourabaya, his ship S.S. Orestes also carrying a few pilgrims—about 140, I think.

We sailed from Batavia on the 22nd July, arriving at Padang on the night of the 24th, and sailed at 9 p.m. on the 25th for Kamaran. I had never been to Padang before, but am pleased to have seen it, as it is a very pretty place. We arrived at Kamaran in Arabia, on the 10th August, and landed all our passengers for Quarantine, and after a beastly hot time, we left on the

18th for Jeddah. We had 14 deaths between Padang and Jeddah, and I only wonder we did not have more, the heat was so intense, it nearly laid all my crew out, and even I, who am a bit of a salamander, had quite enough of it. There were four of our Company's ships in Kamaran, including myself, one had 1,400 pilgrims, two 1,100, and my ship 1,150. However, all good and all evil things come to an end, and it was with thankful hearts we saw the last of our passengers over the side. We all felt younger and better when our stern was pointing Westward through the Reefs at Jeddah, homeward bound, with a clean-smelling ship once more.

# Chapter 19

*1910 Receives award from Mayor of Liverpool—wife ill—
slavery in the cocoa trade—votes for women—family
suffragists speak up—George V crowned—first aeroplane*

During the month of August 1910, and while my wife
and two daughters were in the Isle of Man, my cousin,
William Bryson and his wife (from Chicago, Illinois),
called at my house, and were directed to my daughter's
house (Mrs Dew), and spent the afternoon with her.
The Brysons were on their way to Paris, and expressed
themselves as "being very disappointed to miss me,"
and I was indeed sorry to miss them.

After being home one week, two of my wife's cousins—
Mr and Mrs Stephen, from Norfolk, Virginia, U.S.
America—came and stayed with us for 12 days, and
then went home in the S.S. Mauretania, which sailed on
Saturday, 1st October 1910, from Liverpool to New York.

On the 5th of October 1910, I was presented by the
Lord Mayor of Liverpool (W. H. Williams Esq.) at the
Town Hall, with a handsome pair of Binocular Glasses
and Case, on behalf of the Governor and Community
of the Seychelle Islands, for services rendered to the
survivor of the crew of the Sea Queen, the facts of
which rescue are related in a previous chapter of these
Memoirs. It was a proud day for my dear wife and
daughters, and my Owners were very much pleased with
the presentation, and also my speech in acknowledging

same. They complimented me heartily on saying just the right thing. Personally, I felt like sinking through the floor, and wished I was up at the royal mast-head out of the way, instead of giving a speech to the Lord Mayor and company assembled, amongst which were many of my fellow Shipmasters.

On the second day following the Presentation, the scene changed, and I had to bid Good-bye to my dear wife and family, and go to Glasgow to join my ship, which was sailing on the 8th October from Glasgow to Australia. Before leaving home, I had made all arrangements for my wife to move to a new house, having taken a house, No. 18, St. Catherine's Road, Bootle. I took the house for three years, and we take possession of it on the 1st November 1910. I felt very reluctant to leave the old house, indeed I would not have left it, only on account of the down below kitchens, which are now too much for my wife—I can only hope that by God's blessing, our new home will be as happy and prosperous as the old one.

We sailed from Glasgow for Adelaide on the 8th October 1910, and arrived at the latter port on the 19th November, after a fine passage of 41½ days, sailing again for Melbourne on the 25th November, and arriving there on the 27th November.

I found all my relations quite well, and my cousin— John Michael Goodwin—being at liberty, and not quite as robust as I should like to see him, I took him with me on the voyage to Sydney and Brisbane. At Sydney he was able to stay a few days with my sister Annie, but I could only get out on two evenings, duty having to be attended to. We did not call at Sydney on the way back from Brisbane, but went right on to Melbourne, arriving there on the morning of the 19th December—the trip having done my cousin much good.

During our stay on the Coast of Australia, Great Britain has been in the throes of an Election, the result being that the Parties have been returned in much the same proportion as when the Government appealed to the Country—that is the Irish Home Rulers, and the Welsh Carpet-baggers hold the balance of Power. I was in hopes that we would have had sufficient Unionists returned to take the balance out of their hands, but I did not expect a majority for the Unionists just yet. The Elections in Scotland have been disappointing from our point of view, whether it is the Lords' Veto or Tariff Reform, I cannot say, but I think they are blind to their own interest. There have been a lot of mistakes and blunders made over the word 'Freedom', notwithstanding that the bubble has been pricked over and over again. Look at the United States, and our own Colonies, Protectionist up to the hilt, and more restrictive Laws in their Statute Books than were ever known in England—yet they are always telling us how free they are.

Poor old John Bull! He is always fighting someone else's battle, but his own. Why don't we shout, "England for the English", and send all the damned Welsh Jerry-builders, and the Irish labourers back to where they belong to. An Englishman cannot live in Wales, or Ireland, outside of Ulster, and by the Piper that played before Moses, if I had my way, back they would go. We have given way in every respect, also let them usurp our positions on our Councils and establish parties and Clubs in our towns which profess open hatred of us, yet every damned one of them have had to come to England to earn their living, and to get it they sneak, lie, and beg themselves into our good graces, and then turn and rend us. Why, in my own profession, an Englishman has the life of a dog on a Welsh, or even a Scotch or Irish ship, and they never rest until he is driven out, but I have never known a case where a man, Welsh, Scotch, or Irish, did not get absolutely fair play in an English ship. Why, in my ship at the present moment, I have two Welsh and one Scotch mate, and all the sailors but two are Scotch, Irish and Welsh, and I defy one of them to say one is preferred before another.

*Old England for ever, no power can sever,*
*My heart from the land of my birth,*
*'Tis the land of the free, so it ever shall be,*
*Old England, Old England, for ever.*

The trouble is, we have too much sentimental freedom for our own good.

We sailed from Melbourne on the 26th December, having spent our Christmas Day at anchor in Melbourne Bay, for various reasons connected with ship's business. From Melbourne we went to two small places called Portland and Kingston, and then on to Albany in West Australia, and after taking in 2,000 bales of Wool to complete our cargo, we sailed for Suez on the 3rd January 1911, arriving there on the 25th of the same month. We passed through the Canal quickly and safely, and I may say here, that the passage through the Canal gives me more anxiety than all the rest of the voyage put together, due to the ship taking the ground so often. We arrived at Dunkirk 7th February 1911, and owing to the congested state of the Port, we did not get away until the 17th, arriving at London on the 18th February.

At Dunkirk, I got the news that my wife had been much worse while I was away than I had been led to believe by my Australian letters, but this was due to my missing so many letters in Australia. It appears she got a Chill in the Liver, which laid her up from the early part of November until after Christmas, and then developed Gall Stones, and at the time I was in Dunkirk, they were almost afraid they would have to operate, but I am thankful to say that the necessity for same has passed away. When I got home early morning Sunday, the 19th February, I found she had had an attack on the Saturday, and when I went into her room to see her after Breakfast, I was more than shocked to see how weak and frail she looked, and I am sure she was losing heart, but I am thankful to say that during my short stay at home, there was a wonderful improvement in her condition.

I of course consulted with our Doctor about going away, and he considered I could do so without fear, and I again left home on the night of the 2nd March for Glasgow, there joining my ship and sailing for Adelaide via Las Palmas and Durban, on the 4th March. We arrived at Las Palmas on the 10th March, and sailed again on the 11th, after coaling for Durban, South

Africa. We had a fine weather run to the Cape of Good Hope, which we did not see owing to dense fog covering the land, and so to avoid shipping, and dangers from errors in reckoning, I made what a Devonshire man calls a 'circumbendibus', and so came safely round the Cape and sighted the land at Cape La Agulhas. We experienced a strong current against us up the Coast, even at five miles off the land the current was running 5½ knots an hour to the S.W. However, we arrived at Durban on the 30th March, and there took 1,450 tons of Coal.

The City of Durban is a very clean, bright, and well kept City, reminding me very much of Adelaide. There is a lot of colour in it, Zulus, Kaffirs, Indians, and the good old Britisher, who is always a Britisher in the Colonies, while at home he allows himself to be led by the nose by any Socialistic Labour Radical, peace-at-any-price, Cocoa Manufacturers that choose to lie to him.

We sailed from Durban, or otherwise Port Natal on the 31st March, and hope to be in Adelaide on the 18th/19th April. We were very much disappointed at not getting our home letters at Durban, the mail only arriving three hours after we sailed. In the above remarks re Britishers, I mention Cocoa Manufacturers, meaning Frys, Cadburys, and Rowntrees, who are the principal proprietors of the Radical Free Trade little England press, and apparently the greatest opponents of Tariff Reform and the Conservative Party generally, but will the reader credit that the Cocoa business is the only really protected business in Great Britain, and when one of the Cadburys was taxed with the fact, his answer was, "Oh! no, not protected, the tax is only there to keep foreign Cocoa out of the country"—and when it was also proved that these self-righteous Cocoa Manufacturers were buying all the slave-grown Cocoa from the Island of St. Thome, in the Bight of Benin, West Coast of Africa, and further proved that these slaves—men, women, and children—were flogged to death for very small reasons, and never under any circumstances allowed to return to the main-land, this same degenerate Quaker, who condemned the Boer War and the importation of Chinese Labour into South Africa, as an unjust war, and an immoral slave trade, defended the slave trade in St. Thome as a necessary indentured labour, without which the Cocoa could not be grown for the British Public.

Oh ye Gods! how are the mighty fallen. Just fancy this high-toned moral Nonconformist giving an answer that would do a Jesuit justice. Should my Grandchildren read this, I hope it will teach them to think for themselves before voting, and if they are in doubt, vote Conservative, like their Grandfather. "God Save the King and Constitution."

From Durban to Adelaide we for the first nine days experienced strong Southerly gales, which of course reduced our daily distances, and has so far increased the length of time on the run. The coal we got in Durban was very poor, so owing to the two foregoing circumstances, we made a poor passage to Adelaide, arriving there on the 20th April, and received letters from home, which I am thankful to say gave me good news of my wife, who said she was getting stronger.

We left Adelaide on the 22nd April, and arrived at Melbourne on the 24th. My cousin, J. M. Goodwin met me on arrival, and I spent as much time as possible with him. During the time I was in Melbourne, the people were stirred deeply with an appeal to the Country by the Labour Party to take certain powers from the States, and bestow them on the Federal Government. This took the form of a Referendum, or appeal to the voters to vote straight 'Yes' or 'No' to a certain question, or in fact two questions in separate order.

Now, I am personally opposed to votes for women, because I think women are better out of Politics, and for other reasons which I need not mention here. I am simply mentioning the foregoing as an introduction to my story. Now the women in Australia have the vote, and have formed a National Women's League, their motto being 'For God and Country', and being opposed to the Labour Socialistic Party, they voted 'No' to both questions. My cousin's (J. M. Goodwin) wife, took a leading part in the Local Branch of the League at Box Hill, where my cousin lives, and I being there the night before Polling Day, attended the final Meeting of the League, and I must confess that I was very much struck by the able speeches made by two of the ladies. I was not only surprised, but delighted by what they said, and the way they said it—they were both married ladies, and according to my cousin's wife, they both despised the militant Suffragist in England. Now while I fully enjoyed the Meeting, I was quite aware there was a small fly in the ointment, for my cousin Jack said to me on my remarking that Maggie (his wife) looked tired and worn out, "Yes, I wish this business was over, she is giving too much of her time to it."

On my return to Melbourne some weeks after I found that the fly had grown very big, for the ladies had awakened to the fact that while the wives of the middle classes had by combination won the Election for their class, the Labour leaders had also awakened to the fact, and were organizing their women, and so it became necessary for the Women's League to strive to enrol all the women they could. This meant that Maggie's time—which she had hitherto devoted to her family—was given to Politics, and so the fly in the ointment was stinging damned bad, and the contentment of a peaceful home was in danger of being broken up. Can anyone wonder that I am now more than ever an opponent of Votes for Women. Oh! I would like to give Miss Pankhurst a good spanking.

We left Melbourne on the 29th April, and arrived in Sydney on the 1st May. I saw my sister Annie and family, they all looked well but the son, Ernie, who with his wife and baby was on board with the rest of the family to dinner the night before I sailed. We visited Brisbane in due course, and while there, I had the misfortune to fall heavily on my right shoulder and arm—the accident happened on or about the 11th May, and my arm put out of action for quite a month. Fortunately, no bones were broken, but it was very painful.

We arrived back in Sydney on the 16th May, and after loading a due proportion of cargo, sailed for Melbourne and Adelaide, leaving the latter port for Durban on the 1st June 1911.

While in Melbourne, I of course saw my cousin, Ella Robinson—she, like myself, is getting older, but she looks very well, and I spent a pleasant evening with her at Cousin Jack's house—I also saw my Uncle Taylor and his daughter. They were quite well, and enjoying life on their little farm at Vermont Mitcham, near Melbourne. The old gentlemen is getting very frail, and I fear I may never see him again—93 is a great age. From Melbourne we proceeded to Adelaide, and there had my first long ride in a Motor, some 60 miles through the country. I enjoyed it very much.

We sailed from Adelaide on 1st June 1911, and on the 8th had the 61st anniversary of my Birthday, the ship being in 31° South Latitude, and 105° East Longitude. Birthdays and Christmas Days have been much the same in my life—most of them being spent away from home.

We arrived at Durban on the 22nd June, and found the town en fête, for the Coronation of His Majesty King George V. May God grant him a long and happy reign.

I was very thankful to receive letters from home, and the good news that my wife was getting stronger, and so refreshed by the good news, we sailed again from Durban for London on the 23rd July, 1911, having before sailing received orders from my owners by cable to come home at maximum speed.

I forgot to mention that while in Sydney, I saw an Aeroplane flying over the City. It certainly flew in a wonderfully steady manner, and was looked on by a great crowd of people with interest. It was the first I had seen, and I looked on it with curiosity. It is a wonderful achievement, but I doubt its value to the human race.

# Chapter 20

*1911 Surprises at Dalny—musings on incongruity—
home for Christmas*

On the 5th August 1911, I sailed in the Telemachus from Liverpool for the Straits, Hong Kong, Shanghai, and North China, which means Cheefu, Taku, Dalny, and Chemulpo, the latter being the seaport for Seoul, the Capital of Korea. We called at a new port in the Straits of Malacca called Sweetenham. I call it a port in making, but it is taking a lot of import trade from Singapore, and is becoming a large exporting place for Rubber, but all this will not be of much interest to the readers, who no doubt will think I am a dry old customer, and to tell the truth I am beginning to think so myself, or as the French say, I am getting blasé. Still there is life in the old sea-dog yet, notwithstanding the Rheumatism which has given me considerable trouble lately.

I mentioned above that we called at Dalny. Well, no doubt, dear reader, you will know that this place is the Terminus of the South Manchurian Railway, which in turn connects with the Siberian Railway, by which all good things, and the European Mail, comes to the Far East. Now while travelling to and fro over the face of the waters, I often find myself in incongruous positions, but it struck me that while lying at the wharf at Dalny, we had attained to sublime incongruity, and if you, dear reader, have but a small sense of humour, I am sure you will agree with me, that the S.S. Telemachus lying in a Japanese harbour, in Chinese territory, at a Russian made wharf, lighted by a blatant American Electric Light plant, and the ship discharging English made Locomotives for the Manchurian Railroad, would almost have obtained the height of incongruity, but when you add to this, the chief steward tuning up on a Gramophone, playing anything from 'Abide with Me', to 'Waltz me Round again, Willie', and the audience on the quay, some Manchurian watchmen, coughing and expectorating at the close of each tune, in a most blatant manner, one wonders if they are only relieving their feelings which have been overwrought by the charms of music, or are expressing their contempt for the mad Foreigner. I fear the latter. Oh! shades of far Cathay, how the glories have departed, and been replaced by a measure of incongruity heaped up and flowing over.

Well, all things have an end, even incongruity, so we get our anchor away, and off we go to the Middle East, Chemulpo, arriving there on a good Sunday morning, and instead of Church Bells ringing, up go our derricks and the soothing influence of the steam winches soon begin to play their part in rousing the Heathen from their slumbers—wicked people, wanting sleep on a Sunday afternoon, and a Blue Funnel Boat waiting to be discharged. Oh! the Iniquity of it, stopping a Blue Funnel steamer from moving on. So away we go again, leaving somewhat late in the evening, only to find myself with a thick rainy night in a nest of Islands and strong Tides, calling myself several kinds of fool for leaving that night, but thank God we pulled through all right, though it was a bit of a strain.

We go on to Kuchinotsu for Coals, 2,000 tons of which we take on board in 18 hours, and then off for Yokohama, through the Van Diemen's Straits, arriving at Yokohama on the 7th of October, and leaving again next morning for Kobe, arriving at the latter port 8 a.m. on the 9th October. At Kobe I saw my friends, the Devenishes, and spent a few hours with them, but our stay was only 36 hours, and after loading some 500 tons of cargo, we sailed for Tsingtau [China], in Kianchan Bay, the German settlement. This was my first visit to this port, which has evidently been built as a Naval Depot, and a very fine place our German friends have made of it. They have also built a fine commercial Harbour, second to none in the East, and I was much impressed with the working and facilities of the port. We were only here a few hours, and then off we go to Shanghai.

I cannot help being struck with the fact that though I have been at sea nearly 50 years, I go to a new port almost every voyage, while on the other hand, many ports that I used to go to are now things of the past as far as I am concerned. Change, constant change, has been the key-note of the world during my lifetime.

We remained at Shanghai some three days, and then sailed for Hong Kong, at which port we loaded some 4,000 tons for Singapore in 48 hours. It is wonderful what we can do when we try, but it is damned hard trying to beat time in the tropics.

Having arrived at Singapore, I was told I had to take a batch of Pilgrims to Jeddah. Now the latter is a Turkish port, and Italy and Turkey are at war. I am bound to Genoa, and am carrying cargo which the Turks may consider contraband of war, so I insisted on the Agents cabling to Holts and as they said 'Go', I went. Fortunately nothing happened, but if the Turks had wanted our Manifests, the fat would have been in the fire, and we should have been playing 'Rule Britannia' on a German Sausage.

The evening before we arrived at Suez, we passed The King and Queen on their way to India. Three men-of-war went down first, and then the Medina and a cruiser. Being night time we did not signal, but we felt like cheering them.

We passed through the Canal in Quarantine on account of having been to Jeddah, though we did not in sanitary vocabulary communicate with Jeddah. Nevertheless we loaded and discharged cargo at Port Said, and then went on to Genoa and Marseilles. I had satisfactory letters at both places, and left Marseilles for Liverpool on the 6th December 1911, and the question is still asked, "Will we get Christmas at home?"

We arrived at Liverpool on the 13th December 1911, and on the 21st sailed for Glasgow, arriving the next day, and after I had done the necessary business, I returned to Liverpool by rail, full of expectations for a Merry Christmas—the first that I was to spend with my family for 20 years—and I must say we had a jolly good time over Christmas and New Year—probably the best and most enjoyable time I have ever had in my life. We let ourselves go, and I was as big a kid as any of the company assembled. We also had with us on New Year's

Day a second cousin of my wife's, from Australia—a very nice girl (Ruby Burniston)—and her first time in England. I think she saw how we Englanders can make Christmas and New Year's Day a happy time.

# Chapter 21

*1911 Christmas—reflections on family life—Shanghai—*
*Chinese revolution—news of the Titanic—visits Rouen*

The weather all December was very warm and wet, my wife said it was the mildest season she remembered. While speaking of my wife, I may say her recovery has been a glorious success for Homeopathic treatment, and a credit to Dr Peter Stuart's skill.

Well, all good things come to an end, and I received notice to join my ship on the 5th January 1912, ready for sailing on the 6th for Singapore, Hong Kong, Shanghai and Japan, calling at Jeddah for Pilgrims to Singapore. Owing to very bad weather, which delayed the loading, we did not sail until the 7th, which being Sunday turned out a very fine day. In the meantime I had to pay and receive farewell visits, my two Grandsons being amongst the visitors, and quite proud that their Daddy goes to sea like Grandpa, but they cannot yet assimilate the fact that I am their Daddy's Daddy. The latter is a word I dislike very much, but it is in constant use now-a-days—Democratic, I suppose. What is the matter with good old-fashioned 'Father', I wonder? Well, apart from all this, the Grandsons are fine little fellows, the elder being a very timid but an affectionate boy, whilst the younger one is the opposite, he is bolder and more self-reliant. Neither of them have the salt in their blood; they come of seafaring families on both sides, but they do not seem to care for ships. I do not know whether to be glad or sorry, but I know what their mother and Grandma think. Well, there are worse professions, and better ones, but I thank God it has dealt kindly with me.

Having bidden Adieu to my dear ones, I launched forth on another voyage, sailing on a good Sunday at noon, the weather remaining fine until midnight, and then the wind went South and began to pipe up, and from then until Gibraltar, we had bad weather, mostly Southerly gales and high West sea.

We arrived at Port Said 1½ days late, and found King George and his Queen there, attended by four powerful Cruisers—I and all other loyal subjects were thankful to see their Majesties so far safe on their way home, and I trust they will get home in due course and receive an enthusiastic welcome. God bless them, and confound their enemies.

While passing through the Suez Canal, we hit the bank very hard with our starboard bow, so hard that on our arrival at Suez, I thought it prudent to have her examined by divers, who reported all well, and so after 20 hours unavoidable delay, we proceeded to Jeddah and embarked 817 Pilgrims for Singapore. It is not a pleasant job carrying Pilgrims, and we had not been very long out from Jeddah before Smallpox broke out, and we were only thankful it was not Plague. Fortunately, we did not have more than four cases. After arriving at Singapore, we landed our passengers in Quarantine, had the ship disinfected, and the crew vaccinated, conscientious objectors included, got to the Wharf, coaled, and proceeded on the 12th February to

Shanghai, arriving there on the 21st, after rather a long passage, due to boisterous weather, fog, and tides.

Shanghai. It is wonderful the change in the people. They seem to have thrown off an incubus, and seem more sprightly, more open, and more courteous. Most of the middle class have adopted European dress at last in Shanghai. All have cut off their queues or pigtails, and everyone is wearing European Felt or Tweed hats or caps. This revolution is wonderful, perhaps the most wonderful thing that has ever happened to a race of people. Ten years ago—nay even less than that—our papers were full of the necessity of China awaking from her long period of apathy, and taking her place amongst the Nations of the Earth, but no-one 12 months ago, not even the most sanguine, ever thought the revolution was so close, and that it would only take six months to complete the downfall of the existing state of things, and establish a Republic with apparently so little bloodshed—steamers, railways, and electric telegraph have of course helped materially. The Manchus must have in their self-satisfied way dimly realised the danger of the foregoing, and so opposed their introduction by every means in their power. Of course the ordinary man in the street thinks the Republic is firmly established, and that all the provinces in China are unanimous in their wants and ideas, but excepting only the desire to get rid of the Manchus, I feel sure this is not the case by any means, and peace is being preached when there is no peace.

Already, Dr Sun Yat Sen, the Leader and Dictator of the Republicans is beginning to find out that the ways of a leader are hard. One month ago no-one disputed his orders, now deputations of Citizens are telling him that some of his arrangements are not in accordance with true Republicanism and Liberty, and what they want is Government by the People 'for the People', which means that the human elements (ambition and peace-hunting) are beginning to play, and that every man thinks he could run the Republic much better than Dr Sun Yat Sen. I hear the latter is resigning and I think he is wise, for meddling by the people is bound to come, and then he would either lose his reputation or his head, but if he keeps quiet and plays doggo, the Nation will sooner or later be calling out for him to come back and save the Republic, and he will act Cromwell then if wise. I have no faith in Democracy—a strong man will always and always has led, and I fear there is much tribulation in store for China before things settle down.

Now I think it time to return to my own affairs, though I really do think that the great events which happen in one's life are fit subjects to comment upon even in Memoirs.

After calling at Kuchinotsu, Nagasaki, and Moji, we arrived in due course at Kobe, where we remained four days, and I was able to spend some time with my friends, the Devenishes and Captain Smart. With the latter, I went to see a big Lamplight Procession organized by the Chinese to celebrate the establishment of a Republic and Peace in China. It was a sight worth seeing, and I had no idea there were so many Chinese in Kobe, and I don't wonder that the Police Authorities were so wary about granting permission to hold the Procession. However, all passed off peacefully, but I noticed there were a lot of soldiers with revolvers and swords patrolling the streets.

The irony of the business is that the next morning news came that the Revolutionary troops in Peking had revolted, and were looting the City, and that the President-elect had barely escaped with his life, and for the past week the deliverers of China had been fighting amongst themselves all over Southern and Middle China, killing and robbing their peaceful fellow-countrymen.

Another Republic—Mexico—is now playing the same game, heads I win and tails you lose, and damn everyone as long as I am alright, and yet they cry Peace when there is no peace and never will be in this World until Christ returns to it, and if He never comes, then there never will be peace. Over-population and want of food will always cause men and Nations to fight, and cheap education will breed agitators to keep on the Cause.

We arrived in due course at Yokohama, and after a stay there of ten days, we sailed on the 15th March on the Marseilles, Havre, and Liverpool berth, calling at Kobe, Moji, Tsingtau, Shanghai, Hong Kong, Saigon and Singapore. There is nothing of importance to record, and we arrived in due course at Saigon to load 5,000 tons of Rice, but I may mention that the three next Senior Captains in the Company to myself, are retiring on their arrival home, one of them is a little older than myself, one the same age, and one some two years younger. I am sorry to see them go, but glad they are able to do so, and I sincerely wish them a long and a happy retirement. Their going will have some effect upon my position, but at present I can only wonder what effect it will have.

We finished our loading at Singapore, and sailed from there on the 18th April 1912, but before leaving we received news of the terrible disaster of the S.S. Titanic but the fate of a large portion of the crew and passengers was still doubtful when we sailed, and it was not until our arrival at Suez that we learned to our sorrow that only some 700 people were saved. It is useless to comment upon this terrible disaster; a mistake was made, and from some points of view a justifiable one. The poor man who made it, paid for it with his life and reputation, but two points have again been brought forward and emphasized: Firstly, no unsinkable ship has yet been built, and Secondly, that the man who touches the button is still fallible.

We arrived at Marseilles on the 12th May 1912, and after discharging some 3,000 tons of cargo, we sailed for Havre on the 15th May, arriving there on the 22nd May, after the quickest passage the ship has ever made homewards, and it was very disappointing and annoying to find that the port of Havre was congested, and that no discharging berth could be found for us, and we had to lie six days doing nothing, all of which comes out of our time at home. However, we left Havre on the 31st May for Liverpool, after having enjoyed very fine weather during our stay, and I took the opportunity of visiting Rouen, in which City there are some very fine old Churches and a few very old houses, but most of the old buildings have given way to modern requirements—a pity, but I suppose necessary.

I left Havre on the 31st May, and arrived home on the 2nd June, finding all well and happy.

# Chapter 22

*1912 Meets the Devenishes at Kobe—the Telemachus hits a whale—40,000 people drown in tidal wave*

After a very pleasant, but all too short stay at home, I again sailed in the Telemachus on the 5th July 1912, for the Straits of Malacca, China and Japan, calling at Algiers for Coal. then on to Port Said in the usual way. At the latter place, I received a cable from my owners, telling me of the death of my Chief Engineer's wife, and it was my painful duty to impart the sad news to him. It was the more painful, because we have been together so long—ten years—and I knew and respected his wife so much. She was one of those dear motherly good women, whom every one admired and respected, and I am not ashamed to say I mingled my tears with her husband's over her death. I may mention that my Chief Engineer's name is Joseph Russell.

From the Suez Canal—which we negotiated in safety, much to my relief—we proceeded on to Port Sweetenham, encountering on our passage a strong S.W. monsoon, but no rain, which I fear will be bad for India. While at Port Sweetenham, I went by rail to Kuala Lumpur, the Capital City of the Federated Malay States. Of course it is in the hands of the British. Most of the way by rail, we were passing through Rubber plantations, very interesting, and well worth a visit, notwithstanding the journey, the City itself being worth the visit. The Railway

Station is very fine, and has a jolly good Restaurant, at which we had Lunch and sundry Whiskys and Sodas—the universal drink in the East.

Our next port of call was Singapore, for coaling purposes, and then on to Shanghai, to discharge 4,000 tons of cargo. The weather there was very hot, and the Hospitals were full of Europeans, suffering from heat and various kinds of fevers, but on we go to Japan, and there I learn that my friend—Mrs Devenish—had been operated on for tumour, and had had a very narrow squeak for her life. Her daughter and husband had gone to England, and will probably call on my family—that is, if they can get North.

I learn from Home letters that my family have gone to a place called Robin Hood's Bay—on the East Coast, six miles from Whitby—for their holidays, but I hope the inhabitants and the weather won't be 'a-robbing' them of their just dues and enjoyment.

We sailed from Yokohama on the 19th August for Kobe, and there I spent my spare time between my friends—Captain Smart and the Devenishes—and then on to Shanghai, loading home on the Marseilles-Havre and Liverpool berth, and sailing on the 27th August for Foochow. On the passage down we fell into the right-hand semicircle of a Typhoon, which must have passed over just South of Foochow, about 10 or 20 miles South, but we have no reliable information. What I do know is, I had quite enough of it, and it made me late 24 hours in arriving at Foochow, but I don't complain about that, being only too thankful that we arrived safe and without damage. We stayed in Foochow 24 hours, then went on to Hong Kong, and after loading 1,000 tons of cargo, we sailed for Saigon, thence on to Singapore, at which port we loaded 5,500 tons of cargo, and also took 230 Pilgrims for Jeddah, arriving there on the 3rd October, and sailing on the 5th for Suez and Port Said, sailing from the latter port for Marseilles on the 9th October 1912.

I was very nearly omitting to relate an extraordinary event which occurred on our passage from Singapore to Jeddah. On the 29th September—and a good Sunday at noon—after taking an observation of the sun, I went into the Chart Room with the second officer to put the ship's position on the Chart, the weather being beautifully fine and clear, and the ship off the North Coast of Sokotra [large island in Indian Ocean off N.E. Africa] I had not been in the Chart Room two minutes, when the ship seemed to stop and tremble all over, and before I could get on the Bridge, she again shook all over, and the passengers were all rushing up on the forecastle, and looking over the side. I sent the second officer forward to see what was wrong, but before he got forward, I heard the passengers shouting, "Ikan Bessar" which is Malay for 'Big Fish', and I realised we had struck a Whale, there being quite a number about. On the second officer looking over the bows, he saw and reported a Whale across the stern.

By this time the Chief Officer had got forward, and on his reporting that the Whale had ceased struggling, I stopped the Engines, and went astern, backing clear of the Whale, which sank like a stone. The officers reported he was at least 50 feet long, and that we had struck him on his left side—probably over the heart, thus paralysing him, and the speed we were going at—12½ knots – doubled him across the stern, filling him with water, and drowning him. All this sounds like an old sailor's yarn, but it is true, and furthermore, the whale was across the stern for quite ten minutes—his great bulk reduced our speed to half—five white men and over 100 Malays saw the Whale, so it is no use asking what brand of Whisky we had been using before the happening. Such is life dear Boys!

Well, we arrived at Marseilles in due course, and after a stay of 48 hours, we hove up our anchor, let go the stern lines, and started on our journey to Havre.

Before concluding this brief account of my 21st voyage in the Telemachus I may say that the Typhoon which I experienced on the 28th and 29th of August 1912 passed over a Chinese Town called Wenchow, and is estimated to have drowned 40,000 people with its storm wave. The fact that I was between Foochow and Wenchow, and that a storm centre undoubtedly passed over the land South of Foochow, somewhat puzzled me, but in the light of information since received, I found the uncertainties and doubts cleared up, and I discovered there were two distinct Typhoons. Now the Typhoon which I knew was prevailing East of Formosa, passed North of the latter Island, splitting in two there—one portion travelling about W. by N. and the other about N.W. by N.—thus forming two distinct storm centres, with a 'V' shaped space between them of finer, though stormy weather. I knew I was in the left-hand semicircle of the Northern one—or as I then thought the only one—and was quite easy in my mind, because I was running from the centre, but after sailing some 70 miles, I began to perceive there was something wrong, and the evidence that we were in the left-hand semicircle gave way, and began to point to the right-hand, or dangerous one.

Now it had been my fortune, or misfortune, to encounter on a previous occasion the rare phenomena of two Typhoons travelling in close proximity to one another, and I surmised something of the sort was then taking place, and though doubtful and puzzling, I acted accordingly, turning my ship to the N.E. and steaming in the wind's eye, until full speed on the Engines would not keep steerage-way on her. We took the rest of it as best we could—the centre passing about 40 miles South of us, and just South of Foochow. The Foochow Pilot told me they had a terrible night of it, though they were lying in an unsheltered little Bay. I may say this has been a very bad year for typhoons in the China and Japan Seas, probably the worst for the last 50 years, and I am just wondering if the Indian Seas are going to have their share—the season now being on.

We arrived in Havre on the 23rd October 1912, and I received good news of all at home. Unfortunately we are being detained by the congested state of the Port, thus losing some of my stay at home—that is if I go in this ship.

We left early on the 29th October 1912, and arrived home on the 31st, and found all well. After an interview with my Owners, I learn I am to go in the Telemachus again, and sail on the 23rd November 1912 for China and Japan.

# Chapter 23

*1912 Twenty-second voyage in the Telemachus—
taking pilgrims from Jeddah—a fight onboard—
bad news for the Devenishes—highlife in Saigon*

On the 23rd of November 1912, I left Liverpool in the
S.S. Telemachus—this being my 22nd voyage in the old
ship. We are bound to Jeddah, for the purpose of taking
Mahometan Pilgrims to Penang, Port Sweetenham, and
Singapore. The first night leaving Liverpool was rather
dirty, but afterwards we had very fine weather to Port
Said and Jeddah. At the latter port we embarked 1,000
Pilgrims, and got to Penang without any serious sickness
breaking out, having only eight deaths on the way over.
We had also one birth, and a good old-fashioned fight
between two factions of Malaya—knives, axes, and
sticks were in use, and a little more, and we should have
added to our death list, but on hearing the commotion,
I ran down on to the main deck, and had an axe out
of one man's hand, a stick out of another's and was
in between the two factions before they realised I was
there. Just for a short time I was in danger of having
a knife jabbed into me, but authority prevailed, and
assistance coming to my aid, things quietened down,
and the Doctor's work began. Blood was flowing freely
from arms, heads, and legs, but fortunately there were
really no serious cases. It may be asked, "Why did they
fight?"—and the only reason is the staple one they gave
themselves—"That it was God made them angry with

one another." Verily! God is great, and Mahomet is his prophet!

I spent my Christmas Day in Port Sweetenham, and my New Year's Day in a moderate gale of wind in the China Sea. Later on, the gale increased, and finding my coal consumption going up, I put into Hong Kong for Coal.

We arrived at Nagasaki in due course and there received my welcome home letter, telling me all was well there, and thus refreshed I proceeded on my way to Moji and Kobe. At the latter port, to my very great astonishment, I found that my friends—the Devenishes—had had the misfortune to have their house and contents burned down. Fortunately, they were partly insured, but their loss was great. Nevertheless, Mrs Devenish was bearing up well and doing her best to repair the loss. I also saw my friend, Captain Smart, who is thriving like a 'Green Bay tree'.

After four days stay in Kobe, we proceeded to Yokohama, encountering a gale of wind on our way there, and on arrival hearing that very bad weather was prevailing at home, out in the Atlantic Ocean, and that several wrecks had occurred—I also heard that the Irish Home Rule Bill had passed the Commons. This of course was a foregone conclusion, but the question now is, will the Lords throw it out, and if they don't, and it becomes Law—or I should say part of the Constitution—will the advocates of Home Rule in England, consisting of the large number of Irish in our large towns, go back to Ireland and stay there? To this question I feel sure I can safely answer. No!—and not a damned Jesuit Priest either!

Well, I left Yokohama on the 21st for Kuchinotsu,

encountering a smart gale of wind on the way down. After coaling at Kuchinotsu, we went on to Shanghai, and found it very cold there, freezing every night, and I was jolly glad to get away and begin our journey to milder weather.

We arrived at Hong Kong in due course, and thence went on to Saigon, at which port I was to meet Mr Lawrence Holt [Senior Partner of Alfred Holt & Co] and take him on to Singapore. Soon after we arrived at Saigon, Mr Holt came on board, and told me to pack my bag and come and stay at the Hotel as his guest, which I did, and I must say he gave me a jolly good time—motoring, opera, dining out, and all sorts of good things, which I enjoyed very much, but unfortunately I had contracted a bad attack of Rheumatism in my left knee, and I had to do a good deal of walking when I could have howled with pain. There is always 'a fly in the ointment, and we are all born to trouble, as the sparks fly upwards'. Nevertheless, God is good, and I have very much to be thankful for.

We arrived at Singapore on the 12th of February 1913, and our Mr Holt caught the new ship Ixion and returned to Hong Kong via Manila. People often ask me, "Do you carry passengers?" Well, considering I had 1,000 Pilgrims outwards, and 62 Chinese from Hong Kong to Liverpool—being a firemen's crew for our new Australian passenger ship—I fancy I do carry passengers, not that I am fond of them, but they redeem the situation in the eyes of the people who don't know any better, and who think that you are an old tramp if you don't carry passengers [*i.e.* a tramp steamer, carrying cargo on demand, not regular routes].

We arrived at, and passed through the Suez Canal OK, and proceeded to Marseilles, arriving there on the 12th March, leaving on the evening of the 13th for Havre, refreshed and strengthened by good news from home.

We passed Gibraltar on the 16th March at 3 a.m. having made a good run so far. On Thursday, 20th March 1913, we arrived and docked at Havre. The next day being Good Friday we worked cargo, but Sunday and Easter Monday we will have a holiday, and I fear we will not leave for Liverpool before the afternoon of the 27th March.

I often wonder why I am writing all this, or if anyone will take the trouble to read it. I have my doubts!—but am egotistical enough to keep on doing it. Since I have been on this voyage, our Commodore Captain has retired on pension. As I am now No. 2 or Vice-Commodore, I wonder if it will be my lot to enjoy a pension, or will I get the order of the boot. The foregoing is a reflection, not a memoir, which this little effort professes to be.

I arrived in Liverpool on the 30th March 1913, and to my joy and satisfaction, found all well, and after an interview with my Owners—which was satisfactory—I was granted leave until the ship was ready to sail again for China and Japan.

# Chapter 24

During my stay in Liverpool in the month of April 1913, very little of interest occurred—the usual round of visits and visitors, and the usual amount of growling on my part when either interfered with my desires for a quiet evening, and a good deal of smoothing down by the little Mother. I often feel ashamed of myself, because I get vexed that people don't seem to understand how precious one's time is when home. However, all things have their compensations, and I was much gratified to learn from our Superintendent Engineer that my son was to be promoted to Chief Engineer of the Orestes, in which position I trust he will do well.

Speaking of him, I may mention that he lost his Mother-in-law in a rather tragic manner. She was, or supposed to be, walking alongside the Canal bank at Litherland when she either fainted or died suddenly and fell into the Canal, and was taken out dead. My two grandsons did not appear to miss their Grannie— as they called their mother's mother—but one remark John the elder one made, is worth recording. Seeing his mother crying over the death of her mother, he said, "Are you crying because my Grannie is dead?"

"Yes," his mother answered.

He thought for a moment and then asked, "Has she

gone to Heaven?"

"Yes."

"Is she an Angel?"

"Yes."

"Well, if she is an Angel, what are you worrying about?"

Not bad for a six-year-old. Both the boys are very fine healthy Children, and now the influence of their Grandmother is removed from their lives, I hope they will be more under control. Indeed I see a change for the better in them now.

During my stay at home, my friend, Captain Lowry came over from Belfast, and stayed the night with us. He and I went to see the Grand National run, it was a poor race, but the next day's Steeplechase made up for it, being very exciting and interesting. We were on the Grandstand close to the Winning Post, and so had a good view. Nevertheless I don't think I would trouble to go again, not being interested in racing.

I suppose one must confess that having my salary increased by £60 per year and the privilege of putting £2,000 into the Company at 5% granted to the employees, was something to be greatly pleased about. Yes, and I am very thankful that it is so, but I think the latter privilege should have been granted years ago—if it had, I would have been in a position to retire now.

Well, all good things come to an end, my stay at home included, so on the 19th April 1913, I bid Good-bye to my dear ones, topped my boom, spread my canvas to the wind, and sailed away from Liverpool, on a voyage to the Straits, China, and Japan.

We had uncomfortable, but not bad weather to Gibraltar and Cape Bon; thence to Port Said the weather was fine. We got through the Canal without difficulty, and proceeded on our journey towards Penang, arriving there after an uneventful passage on the 17th May. On completion of discharge of cargo we made our way to Singapore, and so on to our various ports of call, finally arriving on the 12th June 1913 at Yokohama, where I spent five very pleasant days socially, being invited out a great deal. I heard here that the next Senior Captain to myself had been left behind at Hankow, sick, and we have been very anxious about him, but I was much relieved to learn on my arrival at Kobe that he was to be there that day, going home passenger in one of our ships via Vancouver. I went on board to see him on arrival, and found him in good spirits, but very much shaken. He told me he had a touch of the sun and fever, and that his condition had been critical for some days. "I have now finished with the sea", he said, and looking at him I quite agreed, though he is four years younger than I am. I saw my good friends, the Devenishes and Smarts in Kobe, and spent a few pleasant hours with both.

Homewards we called at Shanghai, Hong Kong, and Saigon, at which latter port we took in some 1,500 tons of Rice for Marseilles and Havre, and then proceeded towards Singapore. On the passage I saw the first advertisement about ships going through the Panama Canal, which will not be open before the end of 1914. The North German Lloyd Steamship Company advertise that on the 27th of January 1915, their ship Cleveland will start from New York on a world tour via the Panama

Canal. Passengers are invited to book at once—there is nothing like being the first in the field. Ah! me, what changes have taken place in sea matters in my time. I remember when the idea of the Suez Canal ever being of practical use was laughed to scorn. Indeed my Father, who died the year it was opened [1869] never believed in it being useful, and I shared his opinion then.

At Singapore we embarked 650 Pilgrims, and then went on to Penang to complete our cargo, and to embark 700 more pilgrims for Jeddah, in all 1,350 adults, a nice crowd to have on board a ship for nearly three weeks. The people themselves would be all right, but the amount of baggage which they bring is out of all proportion. Of course, a great deal of it is food and cooking utensils, but they ought to be compelled to surrender half of it to be stowed away in the baggage room. I have talked to Agents until my throat was dry—and had to go to the Club for a Whisky and Soda! All to no purpose. The answer is, if we don't do it, someone else will—Verbum sap. You pull my leg and I will scratch your back.

To ensure a fairly fine weather passage, we took the Southern route to Cape Guardafui, that is from Acheen Head we steered for the 1½ degree Channel, then due West to about Long. 60° E., thence to Guardafui by 'circumbendibus'. We had for the season very good weather, and for the Pilgrims' sake I was glad. We arrived at Perim Island for coal and left for Kamaran the same day, arriving at the latter place on the 1st of August, 14 days 20 hours from Penang. We had three deaths coming over, and one died as we were landing them in Quarantine. Kamaran is a fine Harbour inside, but has a narrow entrance, and the country around is low and sandy—typical Arabia.

At Perim we heard that one of our steamers—the Titan—was ashore at Jeddah. This makes the fourth steamer ashore there in my time, all of which were eventually salved with more or less damage. I wonder if they (the Company) will be as lucky this time. There is no news to be had here, so there is nothing else to do but hope. I am very sorry for the Captain, who I know very well, and I also know how very easy it is to get a ship ashore in the neighbourhood of Jeddah.

On the 3rd August, in company with the Doctor, I went on shore to visit the Pilgrim Camp, and was invited to visit the Research Laboratory, where they examine the blood of suspected patients or persons. I saw through the microscope the microbes of Cholera, Plague, Malaria, Sleeping Sickness, and various other infectious diseases, and what is more, they were handling tubes containing the living microbes of all the above-mentioned diseases with the same sang froid that I would handle a basket of fruit. It made my blood run cold, when one of the assistants brought a basket divided into compartments, and pulling one tube out said, "This is living Plague," and then another saying, "This is Cholera," and so on, in a matter of fact sort of way. He might have been asking which I preferred as a sleeping draught, and any of them would have been quite effective. We arrived at Jeddah in due course, found the S.S. Titan had floated, and had sailed for Suez under escort. After taking our Pilgrims and cargo, we proceeded on our voyage, arriving at Marseilles on the 21st August 1913.

Since leaving Jeddah, my Chief Officer has been laid up, and I have had to keep a watch, which I find very irksome, and a little too much on top of my own work. However, there is no back door at sea, and what cannot be cured must be endured.

We arrived at Havre in good time, though we had a good deal of thick weather during the passage, but nothing eventful happened, and after due discharge of cargo we proceeded to Liverpool, and found all well on arrival, and my wife looking ten years younger, and my daughters quite sunburnt and looking fit after their holidays.

We arrived and docked in the Queen's Dock, Liverpool, on the 2nd September 1913.

# Chapter 25

*1913 Family affairs—overtime pay—*
*beached on the Saigon river—meeting an old colleague*

On Saturday, 13th September 1913, I was called on to take the S.S. Telemachus to Glasgow, and as fate would have it, I got the first dirty rainy night there had been for weeks, but we got there all right, and I came home again on the Monday (15th Sept) leaving my ship in the hands of the Overlooker.

We had beautiful weather during the remainder of my stay at home, and I enjoyed my holiday very much. I may say that I have never known my wife to look so well and robust as she did this last time, indeed the girls also looked well—the only exception being my married daughter, Meg, and she certainly did not look well, and I was not at all satisfied with the account her mother gave of her—but she is married and we do not interfere. My daughter-in-law and her children looked very well, and the latter are thriving and getting on well at school.

On the 16th of September, my Chicago cousin—William Bryson—came over from Paris and right down to Liverpool to see us. He went to my sister first, and then down to us, but we were unfortunately all out, and he left his card to say he was leaving by the 5 p.m. train on his return to Paris. I was very much upset when I got home, and could not understand a man coming so far as he did, and not sending a wire to some of us, saying he was coming—but there you are, 'American rush' and expecting to find everything just as he had planned it. I visited my son's new house (Cecil Road, Seaforth) and was very much pleased with it, being most convenient, and the rooms a good size—indeed it is what I would like when I retire.

Well, the good time is over, and on the 28th September 1913, I bid adieu to those dear to me, and sailed for Penang, Port Sweetenham, Manila, Keelung, and Japan—a slight variation from my few last voyages. We had a very slow run to Port Said, and through the Canal, the weather gradually getting warmer until as the man said—"It is damn hot."

We arrived at Penang in due course, and were there 2½ days discharging some 2,300 tons of cargo, and then we went on to Port Sweetenham, and stayed there another two days discharging cargo. We then proceeded to Singapore to coal, and stayed there overnight, which gave me time to visit some of my friends before proceeding on my voyage to Manila, at which port I arrived in due course after a fine passage. I found a good many changes in Manila, but not so many as I expected to find in ten years, it being that long since I last visited the place. From Manila I went to a place called Keelung in the North-end of Formosa, which was much improved since I last visited it, and the Japanese deserve great credit for the fine Harbour Works they have carried out to completion, thus converting a very unsafe Harbour into probably one of the safest in the East, once you are inside. But the approaches to it in a strong Northerly gale leave much to be desired from a navigator's point of view, though the Japs have done all that is possible in the way of lighting and buoying; but a North-Easter is always attended by thick weather, and as the Chinamen say, "No can see, no can go."

We arrived in due course at Kobe, and there saw my friends, but our time was short, as we always are in a great hurry, simply because we are given an impossible task, that is, to keep dates that are hopelessly lost before we leave Liverpool. However, we jogged along, and in due time arrived at Yokohama—our final port of discharge. We did not remain long, about 50 hours, and if it had not been for one of the Boilers requiring repairs, we should only have had 24 hours stay, so being a free man, I went for a sixty-mile motor ride with some friends. I enjoyed the ride very much, having to a great extent lost my dislike to motors, due perhaps to my understanding them better, and knowing how easily they are controlled.

At Kobe I heard that my daughter Carrie was in bed suffering from a relapse after a bad cold. She was improving, but had to be careful. My eldest grandson was also ill, suffering from Lymphatic swellings. His grandmother says the Doctor considers he is in a bad way. I am indeed grieved to hear this, as he is a dear little fellow.

Well, Shanghai comes next on the list, and there we loaded 2,300 tons of cargo, and were away again in 47 hours. 'Good old hurry up!'

At Shanghai I received a letter from my owners re a subject that has been the cause of much discontent amongst the officers of the Mercantile Marine, viz. the payment for overtime worked. All fair-minded men think they ought to be paid, but our people just beat about aimlessly, and try to put off the evil day. In their letter they say they are "concerned to learn that so much night-work has been done in their ships", making believe they have only just heard of it, and that it must be the fault of the Captains, and calling on them to speed up the days' work, and gain time at sea—then overtime will not be necessary. The Radical liars! But their Great God, W. E. Gladstone, and one or two of the existing Government, were, and are past masters at writing letters of the kind I allude to. The letter was an insult to the intelligence and capacity of their Captains, and is deeply resented by every man in the firm's employment.

Well, we passed through Hong Kong on our way home, picked up a little cargo, and then proceeded on our way to Saigon, arriving there on the 9th December, loaded some 4,000 tons of Rice, Maize, and general cargo, and sailed from there on the 13th, but unfortunately something went wrong with the crank pins, and we had to anchor off Cape St. James, at the entrance of Saigon River, and lay there some 56 hours, trying to get things to run smoothly and coolly. Of course it was a very trying time for the Chief Engineer, for no matter what he did, the low pressure crank pin heated up as soon as he moved the engines. At last we succeeded in getting matters put to right. The ship was in a safe anchorage, so I had personally only the delay to worry about, and I did not do much of that.

We arrived at Singapore in due course, and there loaded some 3,500 tons of measurement cargo. At

Singapore a sad reminder of the past came to my notice. Captain Thomas, who was in command of my old ship, the Diomed, disappeared while at sea when the ship was two days out from Batavia. No-one knows why, and it remains another mystery of the sea. Captain Thomas was Chief Officer with me for two voyages, and in fact left me to take command of the Orestes at Sydney, New South Wales.

From Singapore we went on to Penang, and while there a man came to my door and said, "Don't you know me, Captain Goodwin?"

I said, "No, I cannot call you to mind."

He then told me his name was McDonald, and that he was an apprentice with me in the sailing ship Morna when I was Captain. I remembered the name, but could not recall anything in connection with him. Well, he is the last that can possibly turn up, as all the other boys are more or less accounted for, and yet, perhaps not, for the unforeseen is always happening.

We made a quick run to Suez, and got through the Canal with only one bump at the bank, and after coaling at Port Said, we started for Marseilles, and had the worst passage it has been my lot to make in the Mediterranean, and when we did arrive at Marseilles, we found the place deep with Snow, a most unusual thing there. Indeed it is ten years since it happened before. We remained in Marseilles 48 hours, and then proceeded towards Havre, off which port we arrived on the morning of the 24th January 1914, after a passage which was a great mixture of everything, including 24 hours detention by fog off the Harbour mouth. It was also freezing hard, and I had the coldest night docking I have had for many years. We remained in Havre until the 31st of January, and then sailed for Liverpool, arriving on the 2nd of February 1914, as usual on a good Sunday afternoon. I found all my family well, and my owners pleased with the result of the voyage—I myself being more than pleased when they told me I would be relieved from duty during our stay in the United Kingdom. So here endeth the 24th voyage of the S.S. Telemachus.

# Chapter 26

*1914 Chinese burials—exorcising a ghost—*
*disappointment—pirates of Hong Kong—a theft on board*

After a pleasant time at home, which passed all too quickly, I once again bid Adieu to those dear to me, man-handled my hand-bag, squared my shoulders, marched down the front garden-walk, and disappeared into the darkness of a winter's night—at least that is how it no doubt looked to the dear one who stood on the doorstep watching until the darkness closed around me. Well, I suppose I must come off my stilts, and say that I left home at 11 p.m. on the 20th February 1914, went over to Birkenhead, joined my ship, went to bed, and sailed next morning for Port Sweetenham, Singapore, Hong Kong, Shanghai, and Japan. Our sailing date was Saturday, 21st February 1914, a date I will remember as long as I live, for we had a very dirty night, our Barometer being below 28 inches—to be correct 27.90—the lowest glass I have ever seen in the Northern Hemisphere, and for about six hours the wind simply shrieked, practically attaining cyclonic force. The bad weather continued until we reached the latitude of Lisbon, then we had fine weather until we got past Gibraltar, then the wind came from N.W., strong gale, veering to the N.E., strong gale and rain.

When abreast of Algiers, finding my coal supply was doubtful, I went in for a further supply, and it was the dirtiest day I have ever seen in that port, however 'all is well that ends well', and we got our coal and proceeded to Port Said, the weather remaining very cold and unsettled right into the Harbour and through the Canal, the first comforting warmth coming when we anchored in Suez Bay, which we left at midnight on the 6th March.

Our passage down the Red Sea was a quiet one—four days two hours to Perim, and it was also very cool, at least cool for the Red Sea. From Perim to Port Sweetenham we had a very fair run, arriving at the latter port on the 23rd March, and sailing on the 25th for Singapore, at which port I arrived at 10 a.m. on the 26th, but there being no wharf vacant, we remained at anchor all day, getting alongside at 5 p.m. and commencing work at 6 p.m. and 7 a.m. The next day (27th March) we sailed, having handled 800 tons of cargo, 500 tons of coal, and prepared for and embarked 925 Chinese passengers for Hong Kong. We arrived at Hong Kong on the 2nd April, and landed our passengers, with the exception of one man, who died, and whose body we embalmed, and brought to Hong Kong.

The Chinese have funny ideas about burial, for instance, they put six suits of clothes on this particular body before placing it in the coffin, and then searched the ship for a lucky spot to put the coffin until our arrival in port, finally pitching on a spot just outside the sailors' quarters—I suppose they thought he wanted company—or that the proximity of the sailors would frighten the ghost, and prevent it from walking round and annoying the people in the ship. The Chinese are very superstitious about ghosts—one incident which a

Chief Officer of mine related to me is unique in the way of ghost-laying. One of the Chinese firemen had died, and his shipmates complained that his ghost came and sat with them at meals, and still occupied his bunk at night, and that the ghost must be got clear of, or they would not go further in the ship (I can say that the body had been buried for some time).

The Chief Officer told the men that he would fix the ghost for them that night, and as soon as it became dark, he went into the forecastle, attended by a man carrying a lamp, pulled the ghost out of the bunk, and then beckoned it to follow him, he walking backwards, and the light being carried on ahead to the gangway. My friend then led the ghost down the ladder on to the wharf, and then took a running kick at it, and booted it off the wharf, the Chinese in the meantime following the operation at a respectful distance, and expressing themselves later as being quite satisfied with the performance. Of course it must be quite understood that the whole business was make-believe—but the Chinese regarded it as very satisfactory.

While in the Straits of Malacca, my second officer got an Insect into his eye, which apparently poisoned it, and it was so bad that I had to leave him at Hong Kong, hoping he would be able to rejoin me later on. Of course it is very awkward to lose one of the officers at our busiest time, for it entails a lot more work on everyone, and on me a lot more staying up at night, and also watch-keeping, but it cannot be helped. We arrived at Shanghai on 6th April, and at Yokohama on the 16th, having called at Nagasaki and Kobe on the way up. Nothing eventful happened, and the weather was on the whole fine, but cold.

At Yokohama my old friends gave me a warm welcome, and I passed three very pleasant days there, leaving again on 19th April for Kobe, remaining there two days, and passing all possible time with my friends, the Devenishes and Captain Smart. It is however all rush and go these times, and I sailed for Moji on the 22nd April. There we bunkered and also loaded 2,000 tons of store Coal for Hong Kong. We sailed from Moji for Shanghai on the 24th, and arrived on the 26th, and I got letters from home, they giving the welcome 'all well here' and also that my son's wife, who has given me another grandson, is now about again.

At Shanghai I got a letter from my old friend, Captain Lowry, which contained news which caused me keen disappointment. I had strong—and well-founded—· hopes that I would be appointed Nautical Advisor to our people in Liverpool, having been led to understand that my next Senior—Captain T. Bartlett—was retiring on the ground of ill health, but he has been appointed to the position, his service being longer with the company than mine, and his appointment is both just and good. But financially he did not need it, and I do, to retire comfortably. Of course he had a perfect right to accept the position, but that doesn't prevent me from being disappointed.

My second officer rejoined me at Shanghai, quite recovered, and we welcomed him gladly. After we had loaded some 800 tons of cargo we sailed for Hong Kong, and arrived there on the night of the 30th April 1914, got alongside the wharf at 6 o'clock the next evening, and commenced discharging coal at once—but that won't interest the reader. It may do so however if I record that a bad Piracy occurred a day or two before we arrived. A West River and Hong Kong trading steamer called the Tai-on—under the British Flag, but Chinese owned—left Hong Kong on the 29th April, carrying 400 Chinese passengers. A few hours out of Hong Kong, a portion of the passengers, supposed to number 100 had come on board armed with revolvers, and with the intention of looting the ship, which was supposed to be carrying Specie.

They first attacked the engineer, who rushed for the Bridge, and just managed to reach it with a Pirate close on his heels with a revolver pointed at him. The Captain—who had been lying down—rushed on deck with a loaded Duck Gun and blew the Pirate's head nearly off, slightly wounding the Chief Engineer. The Captain, mate, and two Portuguese Guards held the Bridge against repeated rushes by the Pirates to capture it. They shot some 20 of the villains, who finding such a resistance defeating their plans, deliberately poured Paraffin over the fore-end of the vessel, and set fire to her, she drifting into shallow water, and burning to the water's edge.

Over 250 people were drowned and burned, amongst them being one of the guards, and the Chief Officer. The Captain and Chief Engineer were saved by a Sampan after being in the water for some time. About 150 were known to be saved, 18 of whom (two wounded by gunshots) were detained by the Police on suspicion, the wounded man dying later. A lot of half burned bodies were brought into Hong Kong on the night of the 1st of May by the Water Police.

The Pirates gained nothing but death by their action in setting fire to the ship, but I don't suppose they realised or thought for one moment they were endangering themselves. It is not the first time I have known them to do the same thing. I think when a Chinaman realises that he is beaten, he just says to himself, "Well, if I can't have what I want, neither shall you," but are Europeans free from that sin?

It is 41 years ago since I first saw Hong Kong, and in June 1873 we lay (I being then second mate of the ship Arracan) in Whampoo, loading a cargo of Ginger and Tea. An old Beam Engine steamboat called the Flying Cloud used to run from Canton to Macao and used to pass us every other evening on her way there, and every other morning coming back. One morning she failed to show up, and we all wondered what was wrong when news came that the Pirates had done as related in the recent case, only in the Flying Cloud's case they shot down all the Europeans, and ran the vessel ashore, their Junks being in waiting. They got on board them, first setting fire to the old matchwood steamer, seeing her well alight before leaving her, and abandoning the passengers and wounded Europeans to their fate, a choice of being burned or drowned, either of which happened to most of them. This kind of thing has happened several times since, and nearly always in the same vicinity. In fact the Tai-on was twice looted before, and yet there is never a gunboat near when it happens. The fact is, when the Pirates want to hide, they come to Hong Kong, and it is right there their plans are laid, they being wise to the fact that the Gunboats have gone up River or are in Hong Kong.

Well, time rolls on, and we have to move along. After due discharge and loading, we sailed from Hong Kong on the 4th, and arrived at Saigon on the 7th May. It was very hot while there, and we unfortunately lost one of our Chinese firemen through drowning, he having gone into the River to bathe after being warned by the No. 1 Fireman, who had been told to tell them not to go swimming as the River was very dangerous.

We left Saigon on the 11th for Singapore, arriving there on the evening of the 13th, and after passing the Doctor, we were allowed to go alongside the wharf to coal and work some cargo, returning to the Roads next morning to complete our loading. On the evening of the 16th, we again went to the Wharf to fit out for, and embark 1,000 Pilgrims, which we did, sailing on the afternoon of Sunday the 17th of May for Kamaran and Jeddah. The weather was exceedingly hot while we were in Singapore, and Cholera was getting bad, owing to the season being so dry, and we quite anticipated an outbreak on board during the passage, but thank God we escaped a visitation and reached Kamaran with fewer deaths than usual with such a large number of people on board. After doing five days Quarantine at Kamaran, we went on to Jeddah and discharged our passengers and cargo, and sailed for Suez on the 10th June, arriving there on the morning of the 13th, and after making the quickest passage through the Canal we have ever made, we left Port Said at 5 a.m. on the morning of the 14th June.

I may mention an incident that occurred on our passage from Singapore to Kamaran. We had the Pilgrims on deck for the purpose of collecting tickets, thus leaving their quarters for the most part unwatched, except in such cases where there was a woman or an old man, who it would be cruelty to move. While the people are on deck, some portion of the crew are detailed to clean out the passenger quarters, which are pretty full of luggage. Now there was only one compartment in which there were no passengers on the invalid list, and from this compartment I had a complaint of stealing, and when I mention that the Pilgrims would have with them at the very least £10,000 in gold, besides quantities of silver and gold ornaments, the reader will understand the glorious opportunity for small pilferings on the part of the baser sort; but our robbery was not a small one. Gold to the amount of £60 was taken, the box in which it was kept having been forced open. Suspicion pointed to two of the crew—their quarters were searched, and the result was nil. Now mark the sequel—on the first day of our stay at Marseilles, the Bosun was drunk, and he and a sailor and carpenter left the ship at 4 p.m. Next morning two more sailors were missing, and the whole lot failed to join the ship on sailing two days afterwards. All their clothes were left on board while they had a glorious 'drunk' on the proceeds of the robbery. The bosun and sailor took the money, and the others shared the guilty knowledge of that I am convinced. But I have no proof, worse luck, but as thieves usually fall out there is some hope that I shall be able to learn something later on.

On arrival at Havre I found the missing men awaiting me, they having been sent on at the request of the British Consul—this was a mistake, however the men have to pay up for their fun, but I have not learnt who stole the money.

After a three days stay at Havre, we sailed for Liverpool, arriving on the 3rd July (Friday) 1914—all well.

# Chapter 27

*1914 Outbreak of War—rumours of sea victories—land war begins—Japan enters—Gurkha troops at Marseilles*

After a very pleasant stay at home—which passed with the usual speed—I again had to prepare for another voyage to China and Japan, this time with more than a hint that I should think of retiring.

My last week at home the European situation became so strained that War was threatened in the very near future, and it was with grave misgivings that I left home on the evening of 31st July 1914 to join my ship. We left Dock on the morning of the 1st August 1914, and lay in the River Mersey for six hours, until my Owners decided if it was safe to proceed on our voyage, which we did at noon, with instructions to call at Gibraltar for orders. We had a good run as far as the Straits (three of the Company's vessels in company). There a British Torpedo boat ordered us all into Gibraltar on the morning of the 6th, and before evening there were about 150 steamers, mostly British, and including four captured Germans. Germany declared War—or rather we declared war against them—on the 4th August 1914, because they violated the Belgian Frontier for the purpose of attacking France. News has been scarce, and we do not know what has really happened, but on the 7th August, there were rumours of a big English victory in the North Sea—God grant it is true; but it will not be without great loss to us. We are all very anxious here for confirmation. We also hear that the Germans attacked the Belgian Army, and were repulsed with a loss of 8,000 men and seven guns. I saw the Naval Intelligence Officer to-day (8/Aug/14) and asked if it was safe for us to proceed East, and he said it was not, as two German cruisers were coaling at Messina, and had been ordered out by the Italians, and that our British fleet were waiting for them, so we hope to hear to-morrow that the sea has been cleared of the blighters.

This is the first time I have been ashore at Gibraltar, and I find it a quaint interesting place. I would like to wander round, but two things prevent me—a Rheumatic leg, and Martial Law—two very good excuses. On the 10th, three other of the Company's Shipmasters and myself were on shore, and again interviewed the Naval Authorities, and they said all clear to Malta, so we wired, "Shall we proceed there?" receiving an answer next afternoon, "Proceed Malta." One ship only got away that afternoon, and the others next morning—reason, no pilots, and no sailings allowed between sunset and sunrise. I was the last to get away, not leaving until 9 a.m. on the 13th, being obliged by law to take a pilot in war time—I had to wait until one could be obtained for me—all Eastbound ships leaving together.

On the 12th August, we heard that in the battle of the North Sea, 16 English vessels and 28 to 30 Germans had been sunk, and that the British Admiral and his ship had been destroyed. No further particulars. God grant it has been a victory for us.

Sunday—16th August 1914. We arrived off Malta Harbour at 6 p.m., a blank shot having been fired across our bows by a Torpedo boat. Then the Examination

Officer boarded me, and took one of my crew—a Naval Reserve man—telling me to proceed on my voyage, giving certain instructions as to route.

We learn that England and France are at War with Austria, the latter being the German Ally. Italy is still neutral. The French and British Fleets are over at the Adriatic looking for the Austrian fleet. The officer told me 42 German Naval vessels had been destroyed, and 16 British, and that our Allies were doing well, but no details were forthcoming yet.

We arrived at Port Said at 1 a.m. on the 20th, after a fine run. Still no definite news of the Naval fight, but we hear that the British Troops are on the Continent, having been landed without a single mishap; the Canal being neutral, there are quite a lot of Germans held up. It must be galling to them to see us going on our way, while they are helpless. We were 14 hours getting through the Canal – a good passage—and at Suez we were again boarded by a Naval Officer, who gave me a different account of the Naval battle in the North Sea, than we had before—so which is right the Censor of news alone knows.

I received instructions from the Naval Officer to call at Aden for instructions as to route, and also had to call at Perim for coal. On leaving Perim, a warship – Black Prince—signalled to us that an enemy Warship was somewhere round Sokotra, so I called Aden on 28th August, remaining 24 hours, and was then told it was reasonably safe to go on. We left at 7 a.m. on the 29th. I had never been to Aden before, and was not favourably impressed with it, as a residential place, but it is strongly fortified, and is a splendid Naval Base. I am glad to have been ashore there, though everything was on a war footing, and sentries everywhere. At Aden I heard that our troops had been engaged with the Germans, and after fighting for 36 hours, fell back for strategical reasons. Lord Kitchener in speaking in Parliament said our men had upheld the best traditions of the British Army, and that matters were in a satisfactory condition. All is going on well in England, and the people keeping cool.

We have also heard that Japan has joined in the trouble on our side, and is attacking the German port of Kean Chan. Very kind of them, and well meant, but in my humble opinion, a big mistake. Of course I may be wrong, but their joining us may force Italy to join the other side.

We arrived at Singapore on the 9th September 1914, and were pleased to know that our people were holding their own. Singapore like all other fortified Cities, was full of warlike preparations, and all the volunteers under arms. There are three or four German Cruisers around Java way, and the combined British, Japanese, and French Cruisers are looking for them, but the area to be searched is so great, and the Islands so numerous, that it is like looking for a needle in a haystack. We coaled at Singapore, embarked about 200 passengers, and proceeded for Hong Kong on the morning of the 10th September, and arrived at Hong Kong on the 15th, remaining there two days, then on to Shanghai, Taku Bar, and Dalny, at which port we coaled and received instructions to proceed direct to Shanghai, Hong Kong,

Manila and Singapore.

Dalny is a very fine town, the Japanese having completed the roads and buildings as laid down in the old Russian plans, but it looks like so much money wasted, not on the roads, but the lovely buildings, and apparently no-one to enjoy them, for in spite of the go-aheadism of the Japanese, he prefers his wooden house and Kimono. Of course there are exceptions to the rule, but speaking in a general way, this is correct of our Ally, who are now busy besieging Tsingtau though they are not hurrying themselves about assaulting it, and so save too much bloodshed, which is being so freely spent in Europe.

We left Shanghai on the 10th of September, and the news was that Antwerp was closely invested, and on arrival at Hong Kong on the 13th, we heard the City had been evacuated, but that 24 forts were still holding out good. Our troops and Allies were being strongly reinforced on the French Frontier, and Russia was making good progress on the Prussian Frontier. Millions of men fighting. My God, what a catastrophe! I fear after all is over, Europe will be short of men for many years, and the old Bible prophecy will apply very much, and it will be an honour for a girl to have a man-child out of wedlock. I don't say she won't have honour with a female child, but she will have more with a male one.

From Hong Kong we went to Manila to load 3,000 tons of Hemp for Liverpool, seems a lot, but it doesn't go far in making the Rope required. The news received in Manila was cheering, and from all war accounts the Germans are feeling the strain of the war, while everything is quiet in England and western France.

We left Manila on the 20th October, and arrived at Singapore on the 25th October, and there loaded some 7,000 tons of cargo—principally Gambier [tropical plant with medicinal properties] and Copra.

While lying in Singapore Roads, the German Cruiser Emden actually went into Penang Harbour and sank a small Russian Cruiser which was lying at anchor repairing her engines, then steamed through the Harbour and sank a French Torpedo boat. The German came into Penang disguised as a Japanese Cruiser, and flying their flag, thus taking everyone unawares. This same German Cruiser is a thorn in the flesh. He has sunk some 14 vessels, Indian and China traders, and amongst others Holt's steamer Troilus—a vessel on her second voyage, with a cargo worth £800,000 and the ship £100,000. Nice loss that. There are five Cruisers looking for this Joker, and there was a report the morning I left Singapore (November 1st) that H.M.S. Yarmouth had sunk him. I trust it is true, and I am now running at night without lights for fear of him. I wonder if we will get to Colombo safely.

I may say that the Naval fight in the North Sea mentioned in this voyage's Memoirs, either did not come off, or resolved itself into a Battle between the Arethusa and Torpedo boats, and the enemy's Cruisers and destroyers, a very gallant action, and a victory for us, but not a battleship fight. Since then little has been heard of our fleets, but much of escaped German Cruisers and losses on our side by Submarines and victories also by our Submarines. The Navy has a difficult role to fill, and has been doing it well, as History will no doubt record.

After a week's stay in Singapore, we sailed for Colombo on the 1st November. It is nearly five years since I was there, so I suppose I will see many changes. I arrived at Colombo on the 7th November, and found myself a stranger there as far as the office staff is concerned, and there are many structural changes, in many cases doing away with the old-time Dutch look the town had.

The news from our Army, and from that of our French and Russian Allies was good, and Tsingtau has fallen; but our Naval news was not good for we heard that our Cruiser Good Hope had been sunk, and the Monmouth so badly holed that she had to be beached somewhere off the Chilean Coast, in an engagement with the German Fleet of five Cruisers. This is a blow to our Naval pride, and will have to be wiped out, and our prestige restored. The details are very meagre, and we are not told how much damage the Germans sustained.

We left Colombo on the 8th November, and acting under instructions from the Naval Authorities, we made a roundabout course to Aden, and on arrival there we learnt that we (Great Britain) are at war with Turkey, and that we have knocked out the Forts of Akaba and Babel-mandeb [mouth of Red Sea]. We also learnt to our joy that the Cruiser Emden had been sunk by H.M.S. Sydney, and the Konigsburg had been bottled up by H.M.S. Chatham on the East Coast of Africa. Thank God for that!

We arrived at Suez on the 20th and found the

Canal well guarded by British Soldiers, and that night passage was forbidden. We got through all right, and after coaling at Port Said, and receiving good news from home, I proceeded on my way to Genoa, having on board as passengers, Dr Nicholson and his wife—the Doctor, an old gentleman of 76, used to be our Medical Superintendent, and was going to Cannes to winter, but owing to the War came out to Port Said from Liverpool, joining me at the latter port for passage to Marseilles, at which port we arrived on the 29th November. We sailed again on the 1st December for Liverpool. So far we have been safe from the enemy's Cruisers, but will we be so to Liverpool—we can only hope so. We hear that the Russians are slowly driving the Germans back, and that we are holding them in Belgium. God knows what the winter which is already upon us will bring forth, and it is terrible to think of the sufferings of the men at the front. May God in his mercy give us the victory.

At Marseilles, soldiers—French, British, and Indian—were in evidence all day long, marching to and fro. One Regiment of Gurkhas I saw were marching to the Railway Station for entrainment to the Front, and it did one's heart good to see them marching—but it was sad to think so many were marching to their deaths.

We passed Gibraltar on the morning of the 4th December, and got the word, "All clear to the Lizards" where we were ordered to proceed to Holyhead for our Pilot, arriving in Liverpool on the 9th December—4 months and ten days after leaving.

# Chapter 28

*1915 War continues—Turks in retreat from Egypt—
the Devenishes meet financial loss—Indian regiment
mutiny in Singapore—trial and execution*

Here we are again, on the way out to the Straits Settlements and Japan.

I had a fairly good time home, having both Christmas and New Year's Day with my family. Christmas was somewhat marred by my wife being ill with Bronchitis, and I myself being unwell, but the family and friends had a real good time both days—though we missed some of our young friends, one of whom was in the Trenches, and the other with the Army now training for the Spring Campaign. The War is now five months old, and we cannot yet see the beginning of the end. Indeed until very lately, the pendulum has been swinging both ways, but now it keeps over our way, and I trust that by God's help, it means a flood of victory for us.

After what I may call a satisfactory passage, we arrived at Port Said on the 21st of January, and after discharging 1,000 tons of Coal on Company's account, we proceeded towards Suez. The Canal was practically a fortified Camp, all termini of the Desert routes being garrisoned and fortified, and the Canal Bank entrenched where necessary, indeed wherever it could not be defended by flooding. Armed vessels also were patrolling the Canal, and War vessels stationed both ends. The Turkish Army was said to be within 50 miles of the canal but no-one seemed to mind, being quite sure the Turks and their German friends would get a reception they never dreamed of. We were detained by military orders in the Bitter Lake on the night of the 22nd January, but left Suez Bay at 11-30 a.m. on the 23rd of January, proceeding on our voyage.

I am sorry to say that we got no letters, as the Mail service is all tangled up on the overland routes, so we brought our own letters to Port Said, so to speak. Coming down the Gulf of Suez, we saw the English Warships playing their Searchlights on to the village of Tor, which is the Coast Town on the Caravan route from Sinai and Akaba into Turkish Territory. There was also a Guard-ship at the mouth of Akaba Gulf. In the middle of the Red Sea, we passed at night a large convoy of Troopships, bound North—more Australians for Egypt I think, understanding they were about due to arrive there.

We arrived at Penang on the 9th February 1915, and received news of the Turkish attack on Egypt which absolutely failed, and the Turks were in full retreat. We also heard of action in the North Sea between a German Battle Cruiser fleet, and a British one. The Germans who were crossing the North Sea on a raiding expedition on the English Coast, were intercepted by the British, and a running fight ensued, our ships steaming 29/30 knots in pursuit of the Germans, sinking one and badly damaging and setting on fire two others, which escaped into their own Minefield.

On leaving Penang we passed close to the wreck of the

Russian War ship which was sunk by the German War ship Emden. Speaking of her the Pilot told me several gruesome stories of the disaster. He also told me of one Russian sailor who had one leg torn off, and yet swam ashore a distance of half a mile. The Pilot said pieces of bodies were floating about all over the Harbour, and concluded by saying, no-one will eat fish in Penang, because large quantities of them were feeding on the bodies. The point to us was that we had all had fresh Fish for Breakfast three hours before the Pilot told me the story, but knowing that few people have as strong a stomach as myself, I did not tell anyone on board, but we had prawn currie for Breakfast next morning, the Prawns being bought in Penang! We could not have the currie wasted, could we?

From Penang we went on to Port Sweetenham, remaining there about 26 hours, and then on to Singapore for Coal, arriving there at 7 a.m. on the morning of the 13th February, and left for Nagasaki at 5 p.m. same day. Our passage to the latter port was uneventful, but we made rather a quick run up.

From Nagasaki we sailed for Kuchinotsu, and after loading 1,600 tons of bunker coal, we proceeded to Moji to discharge some cargo, leaving there on the evening of arrival day, Feb. 25th, and arrived at Kobe noon of the 26th. I found most of my friends in good health, but all eleven months older than when I last saw them; to the young ones that doesn't count, but it does to the older ones. The War also has made a difference, many having gone home to defend the dear old Motherland.

My chief friends—the Devenishes—have met with

financial loss, principally from being too trusting. Fancy trusting or lending a man £1,000 and never getting a receipt for it—stupid folly, I call it. Naturally he clears out, and the money is gone, but damn his eyes, it was the Widow's all. Nevertheless I am very sorry for Mrs Devenish, whose goodness of heart led her to trust her son-in-law—who is the culprit—and he knew that he was taking the Widow's mite. Now he is in America, leaving behind him a young wife of 25 years of age, penniless and a Bill of Sale on her furniture, but thank God, childless. The young whelp skinned them of everything, even to the money for his passage to the States.

After two days stay in Kobe, we went on to Yokohama, remaining there five days, and then returned to Kobe, arriving on the morning of the 6th March, and sailed at 2 p.m. on the 7th March, for Kuchinotsu, to load 3,000 tons of coal for Singapore. I spent the evening of the 6th with my friends—the Devenishes—and bade them what may be a last Good-bye. I am referring to my probable retirement this time home.

We arrived at Kuchinotsu in due course, and after loading our coal, we proceeded to Shanghai—the German Lye [caustic soda] Factory—and found the weather very cold on arrival there, which was on the 13th March, but the Lye Factory was running as hard and hot as ever. We loaded some 2,000 tons of cargo for Genoa and Liverpool, but it puzzles me how we are going to get to Genoa, as all we have loaded is contraband according to the new declaration of the British government, which did not reach us before I had loaded. Of course it is for a neutral Country, and as far as I know honestly meant for the use of neutrals. If I thought otherwise, I would not carry it, but things will develop later on—in other words, 'Wait and see'.

We left Shanghai on the 15th of March for Hong Kong, arriving there on the 18th March, and after filling up with Soma [Middle-eastern intoxicant plant] and Coast cargo for Singapore we sailed on 20th March and arrived on the 25th.

I have not mentioned that two days after I left Singapore, the Indian Regiment, the 5th Bengal Infantry, which had replaced the European one as Garrison Troops, mutinied, and some 40 civilians—European, and a few Malays, and some Military Officers—were shot dead. All the volunteers were called out, and all Europeans were made Special Constables, and armed with Rifles, having orders to shoot armed Indians on sight. Some 400 men mutinied, and came down on Singapore residential quarters in two bodies, bent on killing the English and looting their houses. Fortunately, a small sloop of war called the Cadmus was lying at the wharf. Her crew consisted of something like 80 men. They were all landed at once, some Motor Lorries commandeered, Machine Guns were mounted, and they set off to meet the nearest lot, which they quickly dispersed and chased into the Jungle.

The other party of Mutineers marched to the German prisoners' camp, killed the Guards, who were taken by surprise, and then released the prisoners, or told them they were free. About 15 took advantage of the opportunity, and tried to escape, but only seven managed it, seizing a large sampan and escaping to Sumatra. Those who did get away were the worst of the lot, some of the Emden crowd, and the head of a large firm in Singapore called Benn Meyer, who had been sentenced to seven years imprisonment to begin at the close of the war for espionage. This Joker had the nerve to send the Governor of Singapore a telegram from the Dutch office, to where he escaped, saying he had arrived quite safely after a fine passage.

The Government have kept matters quiet, or at least have called the Mutiny a Riot, but it was the real thing, and the Navy saved the day, everyone acknowledging that. Well, to cut the story short, they had them (the Mutineers) all rounded up, either dead or alive, and the trial by Court Martial of those taken with Arms and Ammunition began. About 20 were shot before I arrived back to Singapore, but the day after my arrival the sentences upon 45 of them were promulgated outside the jail, the wall forming one side of the square, a territorial Battalion another side, volunteers in front and Garrison Artillery on the fourth side, while 100 volunteers formed the firing party drawn up in two lines.

Then firstly 23 men were led in and their sentences were read out loud, some got life, and some for other terms down to five years penal servitude. They were then marched off under a strong escort of Sikhs and European soldiers, and the death-sentenced men were marched on with their hands tied behind them, and a strong force of Warders dressed in white, and armed with rifles. The prisoners—22 in number—were placed with their backs to the wall, and their feet made fast to

242

stakes previously prepared. Their sentences were then read out, each man being named. The officer reading their crimes, concluded with: "They have broken their oath to His Majesty the King Emperor, they have been untrue to their salt, and they are sentenced to be shot dead—thus justice is done. Firing party, Attention. Front rank kneel, load, present, fire!"

Twenty of the blighters fell as one man, calling on the name of 'Allah'. Two wavered for a few seconds, and quickly half a dozen shots rang out, and they pitched forward on their left side face. A Doctor, and two Warders—the latter armed with revolvers—went down the line of dead and dying men, and at a sign from the Doctor, the warders gave those still alive their 'coup de grâce'. In all about a dozen shots were fired, one man taking three before he passed in his cheque. It was rumoured that the Chief Warder, whose son was shot dead while guarding the German prisoners, rather enjoyed giving the Jokers their quietus.

A great majority of the German prisoners remained quiet, recognising the futility of trying to escape, though the Mutineers threw their arms into their compound. It is however generally understood that German money and intrigue, through Arab Agents, was at the bottom of the trouble, though the Authorities have observed strict silence on the subject. Nevertheless the same thing very nearly occurred in Rangoon; 500 men of a Beluchi Regiment [from Balochistan, now Pakistan] had to be disarmed and tried by Court Martial, 200 were sent to Calcutta Jails, and 200 to Madras. To the observant man it appears as if the whole scheme was to rouse the Mahometan world against England, and I think our Government know that India is not to be trusted without White Troops, any more than Ireland is without English troops. This applies to a small minority of course, but minorities have a way of sticking their heads up like a 'Jack in the Box', and the loyal people are not supported as they should be according to the political Party in power.

The Regiment which mutinied in Singapore—the 5th Bengal Infantry—was one of the few Indian Regiments which remained loyal during the Indian Mutiny in 1857, and strange to say one of the Havildan Sergeants, who was shot for mutiny in Singapore, was the grandson of one of the Sepoys of the Regiment who remained loyal, and who was rewarded by the Government with a plot of land, medals, and a money grant. Sad in its way, was it not, oh reader? but common enough in History.

There has been a lot of surprises sprung upon us from home over the War. The bombardment of the Dardanelles, sinking of British and neutral ships by German Submarines, and various other happenings, the knowledge of which makes a passage of only a few days tedious, owing to our desire for news.

We loaded full up at Singapore, being there eight days, and sailed on the 3rd April for Suez. On the 17th Inst., at midnight in the Red Sea, a passing vessel morsed us as follows: "A battle has taken place in the North Sea, 23 Germans sunk. We have passed through the Dardanelles."

The next night another vessel morsed: "Dardanelles forced, we are doing remarkably well on land".

Good hearing, but it has only whetted our desire for

more details, and we shall be disappointed very much indeed if the report of the Naval Battle turns out to be a rumour.

Well, we arrived at Suez April 20th, and found that the above was nearly all flim-flam. There had been no North Sea battle, and we are not through the Dardanelles, but have done fairly well on land. We don't know the names of the vessels who gave us the news, but we should like to punch the fellow's head who gave it to us.

At Suez we had a sandbag bulwark put round the Bridge, to protect us from snipers while going through the Canal, but we got through all right. We however tied up at a Station before Ismailia, where there was a camp of East Lancashire Territorials and Gurkhas, and as we remained an hour there, some of the soldiers came on board, and also two officers, a Captain, and a Lieutenant of Gurkas, both jolly fine fellows, who I had the pleasure of entertaining, and who entertained me with an account of the fight with the Turks, which both of them were in.

We got through the Canal all right, and after discharging and loading more cargo, we left Port Said at 6 p.m. on the 21st of April, and arrived at Genoa on the 26th at 5 p.m. and learnt that the Anglo-French troops had been landed at the Dardanelles under Command of General Ian Hamilton. We also heard that the Germans were making another attempt to break through to Calais; fancying they could not do so by direct fighting they used poisonous Gas, which enabled them to gain some ground – Brutes!

We sailed from Genoa on the 29th April, arriving at

Marseilles on the 30th, and were detained there six days owing to the Port being congested. However, we got our cargo discharged, and sailed on the 6th May for Liverpool. May our Heavenly Father bring us safely through the War zone.

After a good run from Marseilles, the best indeed that I have ever made, we arrived safely in Liverpool on the 13th May, and found all well at home, but we received news of the torpedoing of the S.S. Lusitania on the 7th May and the loss of 1,300 lives—a dastardly performance by a German Submarine. I trust we shall be able to catch the blighter who did it.

# Chapter 29

*1915 Last voyage—28th voyage of the Telemachus—*
*the ship fitted with retro gun—sees typhoon wreckage—*
*an old friend passes away—retirement*

After my arrival home on the 13th May, I was advised by my owners that the ship would load in Liverpool, or rather Birkenhead, and sail on the 5th of June for the Straits and North China, but owing to shortage of labour we did not sail until the 13th June.

During my stay at home, I had the sad duty of going up to Glasgow to the funeral of an old Bangkok-Singapore friend—Mr J. Inglis—and I still have the sad duty of meeting his sons at Singapore, and telling them all about it. My time at home was otherwise very pleasant, my wife strong, and my daughters in good health, and the weather perfect from a holiday point of view. I enjoyed every minute of it. My son was at home, and that added to our enjoyment. Yes! we had much to be thankful for, and I trust we were. I also had my 65th birthday anniversary at home. I can hardly believe it myself, for I don't feel any different than I did at 40 years of age.

A week before I sailed, I was advised that my ship was being fitted with a 4.7 gun astern, for the purpose of making a running fight with German Submarines should we be attacked. Two R.N. Artillery men were placed on board as gun-layers, and the crew formed the rest of the gun crew and ammunition passers. We left

Liverpool on the 13th of June, and passed Gibraltar on the evening of the 17th, just 4 days 11 hours passage, which passed without incident. I may mention here that my son sailed from Liverpool on the S.S. Orestes on the morning of the 12th June. She had a cargo of Coal on account for Port Said, and goes from there to Java for homeward loading. I passed his ship on the 19th June, and signalled, all well.

The weather has been very warm for the Mediterranean, indeed I have never known it so hot before, and suppose that is because of the War. Speaking of the latter, we are now getting anxious to hear how our people are doing in the Dardanelles, as well as in Belgium and France, that means we are very anxious for news. God grant it may be good.

We arrived at Port Said on the 24th June, and heard nothing, or very little War-news—small advances in France and Belgium, also a little improvement in the Dardanelles. I must however say that we heard of the attack on Karlsruhe by our air fleet, an answer to the Zeppelin raid on London, only very much more successful, because it caused the Kaiser to say, "His heart bled for his beloved City, suffering from the ruthless enemy attacks"—quite a good sample of the 'pot calling the kettle black'.

We discharged our Gun at Port Said, and fortified our Bridge with sand-bags for the passage through the Canal, and left Suez on the 25th June, and after a quick run we passed Cape Guardafui, and so into the Indian Ocean, and at one time dreaded S.W. Monsoons, which we found very strong—there were little drops of water flying about all over us.

A rather amusing incident which at first looked like tragedy occurred on the morning of the 2nd July. The Chief Engineer reported that the Firemen's boy who was last seen at 6-40 a.m. was now missing. A strict search was at once instituted, but no sign of him could be found, so we concluded he had committed suicide. His effects were collected, and his disappearance duly entered in the official Log, and when everyone had become reconciled to his loss, and I was lying down taking my afternoon sleep, the Chief Engineer knocked at my door and said, "We have found the sheep which was lost."

I answered, "Take him out and kill him, and bring his remains to me at 4 p.m."

The blighter had felt tired and stowed himself away to have a rest. Damn him! he gave me a lot of writing for nothing.

We arrived in Singapore on the 12th July, Orangeman's Day, and I, or the ship, went into the new Dock for the first time, and a very fine Dock it is. There was not much war news, all hands pegging away, but not much progress being made. The Kaiser says he will finish the War in October. We say, "Perhaps, and perhaps not." My young friend – James Inglis – came to see me on arrival and I had to tell him the sad details of his Father's death.

We sailed on the 14th July for Hong Kong, with 315 passengers on board, and had a pleasant run up, arriving there on the 19th July in good shape, as our American cousins say. The weather was very hot in Hong Kong—of course July is the hottest season—and in spite of my knowing all about it, the heat distressed me somewhat. Am I growing older or weaker? Whatever may be the cause, I felt it very much. After a two days stay in Hong Kong, I sailed for Shanghai and made a quick and pleasant run up. Typhoon conditions were present, but only the preliminaries, heat and low barometer, but we did not get anything until the 28th July in Shanghai, when the right wing of one visited us, and did a fearful lot of damage on the water front. I never saw such a scene of wreckage. The Banks of the River were one mass of wrecked Junks and steam launches, workshops and trees blown down, houses unroofed, and God knows—for no-one else will ever know—how many Chinese boatmen and Riverside dwellers were drowned, whole families must have been wiped out. Two big steamers and several small ones were ashore, but I am thankful to say we escaped injury, being fast to the strongest Wharf in Shanghai. I don't know the full extent of the damage, for I sailed the next day for Taku Bar, and on arrival there they told me all the wires were down and they had had no communication with the South for some days.

We left Shanghai on the 29th July, and arrived on the 1st of August at Taku Bar, after a passage of dense fog all the way. It was very tiring, still I have known myself to be much more tired than I was on arrival, and 725 miles of fog navigation is no joke at any time. I found Taku Bar and the people there just the same, and after due discharge of cargo, we 'topped our boom, got the anchor a short stay peak, filled on our fore topsails, and bore away for Dalny'—in other words, we hove up our anchor, put her full speed ahead, and sailed for Dalny at which port we discharged our cargo, bunkered, and sailed for Kuchinotsu on the 5th August, and there took in 2,000 tons of Coal for Singapore stocks, sailing again at midnight on the 7th for Shanghai. Quick work, but 'We are all bound together with a grey goose feather, and the land where the grey goose flew'—Old England!

We arrived at Shanghai on the 9th August, and sailed again on the 12th for Hong Kong, arriving on the 15th August. Well, the War news if not startling, is at least comforting. Things seem to be shaping our way, thank God. I am bringing home a young man from our Wharf Office at Shanghai, who has been recommended by the Consul for a Commission in the Army. He is a trained man. After taking in some 700 tons of cargo, we sailed from Hong Kong on the 16th August for Singapore.

This voyage has passed very quickly indeed. It is the quickest I have made for many years, owing to our not going to Kobe and Yokohama. I hear that an old friend at the latter port—Captain James Martin—has passed away from us. He was a good fellow, and I had a very great regard for him. He was about 72 years old, and I hear he passed quietly away in his sleep. I trust to hear particulars from his brother shortly.

We arrived at Singapore on the 21st August, discharged 2,000 tons of coal and 500 tons of cargo, and then loaded 5,000 tons of cargo consisting of Wool, Rubber, Pepper, Sago, Flour, Timber, Gambier, Copra, Tin, and Preserved Pines in tins, with various other odds and ends, such as Spices and Hides. The news from home of the War—well, one cannot say it was good, still there were hopeful signs.

We sailed on the 26th August, and arrived at Port Sweetenham on the morning of the 27th, and after loading 8,160 cases of Rubber, we sailed that evening for Penang, arriving there at 2-30 p.m. on the 28th August, loaded 1,560 tons of cargo, consisting of Tin, Rubber, Copra and Pepper, and sailed again at 11 a.m. on the 29th August for Colombo, to finish loading.

We arrived at Colombo on the morning of the 3rd September, and there discharged 700 tons of Rice, and about 100 tons of Penang Rubber, and then loaded 1,800 tons measurement of Tea, Rubber, Coconut Oil, and Fibre, also a large quantity of Desiccated Coconut, sailing again at midnight on the 5th September for Suez. Martial Law had just been declared when we arrived at Colombo, which is a sign that the Authorities have the situation well in hand, and the natives have been taught a lesson they won't forget in a hurry. Quietly it is said, about 4,000 to 5,000 natives were shot during the trouble. Of course the Government don't admit so many, but all Governments are prevaricators of the truth. They have to be, and rightly so when occasion demands it for the Public good.

During my stay in Singapore, we heard that my old ship the Diomed was sunk by a submarine while on her way out East. The Captain and two others of the crew were shot and seven drowned. So far as we can learn, this took place off the S.W. Coast of Ireland. The Captain was an old second officer of mine—his name was Miles.

After leaving Colombo we had firstly light monsoons, and then strong to Cape Guardafui, but during the light part we experienced that peculiar and rare phenomena—White Water— that is the whole sea in our visible horizon was white like milk. At night it has a most weird appearance, and no man can tell what it is, whence it cometh, or whither it goeth. The weather was very hot in the upper part of the Red Sea, and we are all looking forward to getting into the Middle Sea.

We arrived at Suez on the 17th, and found little or no change in the Theatre of War. Much fighting and meagre results, but the Russians have retired out of Poland, some say defeated, others say strategical movements—a little of both I think, anyhow it is an anxious time for the Allies.

We left Port Said at 10 a.m. on the 19th September for London, via Plymouth, and experienced very hot weather as far as Algiers. On the 23rd we had a nasty accident—two firemen fell down the engine-room, one broke his thigh, and the other cut his head badly. No Doctor—so I had to sew up the man's scalp and set the broken thigh. Nice entertainment for me. All the years we have carried a Doctor, I have never seen one of them have one quarter as much work—medical or surgical— as I have had this voyage.

September 24th, at 5-45 a.m., Lat. 37° 32 N. Long. 6° 8 E., sighted a two-masted (Black Funnel) East bound steamer bearing E.S.E., distance about three miles, with what appeared to be a Submarine following close astern of her. My Chief Officer and Gunner both reported that they saw flashes of light from the submarine, apparently from gun fire. The steamer was smoking up good, but we lost the submarine before our distance warranted us doing so, she having been in sight quite twenty minutes. We saw no National colours hoisted.

Nothing of interest occurred during the remainder of our passage to London, and in due course I got down home to Liverpool and found all comparatively well, colds being the order of the day.

After reading over these few Memoirs, I wonder what interest they will ever have for others. Yet, they are the Memoirs of a man who has seen sailing ships almost pass away—wood, and then iron, also steamers develop from 700 tons to 30,000 tons, and they in turn developing into a cheaper and better method of propulsion, and that also being overshadowed by aeroplanes, and/or air navigation. When I look back on the more than half a century of sea life, I can only feel amazed at the changes I have seen.

On going for the usual interview with the Directors of the Company, they expressed great satisfaction with my services during the years I had been in their employment, but strongly suggested that I should retire for my own sake. Well, they put it so strongly that I knew they meant me to go, and as I had a clean record, I thought it better to take the hint and go, and on the 12th October 1915, I handed them my resignation, they on their part saying they would deal generously with me, and according to their lights, they have done so.

I may say the wrench was great, and I felt it very much, but afterwards I was glad, and content that I had retired, and I certainly feel thankful to our Heavenly Father for all the blessings and memories vouchsafed to me during a long and successful sea career. As for the rest of the acts of J. H. Goodwin, Master Mariner, are they not written in the book of the Recording Angel.

Amen!

# As Seen By Others

# British Steamer Takes Immense Cargo of Valuable goods

*[Article from an unknown American newspaper regarding the cargo of the Telemachus in c1910]*

Blue Funnel Liner Sails This Morning For Liverpool Loaded to Capacity

Carrying the most valuable cargo of American products that was ever sent from the Pacific coast in the British steamship Telemachus, Captain J. H. Goodwin, of the Blue Funnel fleet, sails from Tacoma at 8 o'clock this morning. Her destination is Liverpool, via Japan, China, East Indies, the Suez canal and the Mediterranean, the longest steamship route in the world.

In her immense hold the Telemachus has 12,000 tons of freight, valued at $1,530,287 [approximately US$37,324,070 today]. In all this great amount of merchandise there is not one pound of contraband, all offers of this character having been refused.

The Telemachus arrived on Puget Sound about ten days ago. She discharged cargo at Victoria, Vancouver and Seattle, arriving in Tacoma Sunday, since which time most of her outboard freight has been loaded. The liner was late in reaching this port but she was given unusually quick dispatch, considering the size of her cargo, and she sails on time.

Yesterday the longshoremen had a busy time at the

257

Oriental dock and it was late in the night before the last pound of freight had been lowered into the hold. The vessel was cleared at the custom house last night and a glance at her manifest proves that there is a demand for American made goods in the Orient and England. Besides the goods consigned to Japan, China and Great Britain, not an inconsiderable amount goes to Australia, India and New Zealand.

The most valuable portion of the Telemachus's cargo consists of domestics and sheetings, millions of yards of which go to Shanghai and Tientsin to be made into clothing for the almond-eyed population. Salmon by the thousand cases is on the manifest, consigned to nearly every port at which the Telemachus touches. Condensed milk, flour, canned meats, groceries and other staple articles are to be carried thousands of miles. American machinery, drugs, medicines and electrical supplies are in the cargo. An American typewriter is on board for the Orient. Tacoma lumber forms a portion of the freight, while there are numerous other American manufactures.

Distinction To Be Proud Of

The manifest of the big liner shows that in domestics, sheetings, flannels, salmon and flour she carries merchandise worth $1,433,989. The rest of the cargo is general cargo. This is a most valuable cargo and it will likely be many months before this record is equalled in Tacoma, and will be as long before any other Pacific port makes a better showing. The Telemachus has brought to this city a distinction of which Tacoma may be proud.

Captain Goodwin, master of the Telemachus, is a well-known mariner, who has been in Tacoma before in Command of the big freighter. Captain Goodwin is a genial fellow, who has made many friends in this port. He is considered one of the most trustworthy navigators in the employ of Alfred Holt & Co, the owners of the Blue Funnel and China Mutual steamships.

Where The Cargo Is Going

In detail the manifest shows every bit of freight which is carried by the Telemachus and the cargo consigned to the various ports, with the value of each lot, given below:

Liverpool

39,218 cases of canned salmon, valued at $286,543

London

40,213 cases of canned salmon, valued at $298,462: six packages of personal effects, $375; four cases hosiery, $700; one box wood samples, $20; two boxes mowers, $150; three packages household effects, $500; one case personal effects, $100; seven bales raw furs, $18,539; 60,560 pieces of rough lumber, $750.

Devonport

40,540 feet lumber, $550

Glasgow

Two shafts and tubes, $450; one box machinery, $135

Freemantle

2,072 cases of canned salmon, $14,128; 40 bales hops, $2,235

Liverpool or London

3,189 cases canned salmon, $23,460

Albany, West Australia

310 cases salmon, $2,325

Singapore

Two boxes canned salmon, $15; five packages canned meats, $35

Penang

One box canned meats, $7

Kobe

Four cases hardware, $200; 12 packages groceries, $75; 26,000 sacks flour, $26,000

Yokohama

Personal effects and supplies, $175; 66 bags talc, $125; seven bales drugs, $780; 22,762 sacks flour, $26,000

Shanghai

16,292 bales domestics, flannels and sheeting, $718,390; one typewriter, $100; photographic material, $230; six boxes electrical machinery, $430; eight cases medicine, $220; 24 hogshead leaf tobacco, $4,090; 220 cases cigarettes, $16,055; 614 boxes Washington apples, $14;

111 cases copper ingots, $6,095; 350 cases condensed milk, $1,820; 57,455 feet lumber, $675

## Hong Kong

560 cases condensed milk, $3,185; 16,652 sacks flour, $16,652; 50 cases cigarettes, $3,640; 10 cases smoking tobacco, $750; 113,654 feet lumber, $1,300

## Moji

5,000 sacks flour, $5,000

## Brisbane

15 bales hops, $790

## Adelaide

250 cases canned salmon, $1,560

## Sydney

790 cases canned salmon, $5,530

## Townsville

100 cases canned salmon, $700

## Chemulpo

400 cases condensed milk, $2100

## Nagaski

70 cases condensed milk, $365; 150 cases milk, $665

# "Ship Subsidy Will Not Do", Says Captain Goodwin

*[This short piece among John Goodwin's papers is a typed copy of an interview he gave to an American newspaper during a stop-over in the USA, c1910]*

Veteran Mariner Comments Forcefully Upon Decadence Of American Merchant Service

The recent report of American shipping to the Philippines calls attention again to the decline of the American Merchant Marine. As a commercial Nation, the United States sends her products to the marts of the world – but in foreign bottoms.

Secretary Hay's remarkable diplomatic success in securing the opening of two ports in Manchuria is of the utmost significance to the manufacturers of this country, but of comparatively none to the American shipowner. The latter's ships are all busily engaged in other traffic, and their number is so small, that they cannot begin to even adequately care for what they have.

Captain J. H. Goodwin of the huge freighter Telemachus—now in port in discussing the situation today, said:

"The English nation is the common carrier of the World's goods to the Orient. This is not my opinion merely because England is my mother-country, and I am the Master of an English ship, but it is an undeniable fact. We have no fear of the American as a competitor in the transportation trade to the Eastern market, but our strongest and greatest rival is the German.

"Unless one has followed the sea for 40 years, or more, as I have, and noticed the appearance of new vessels flying the German flag, he will but little realize the rapid strides of the German Merchant Marine, though he may be more amazed at it when the facts are presented.

"The decadence of the American Merchantmen is well exemplified by the presence in this port of my ship, and the Kosmos Liner, Herodot, lying but a few wharves from here. My big Blue Funnel liner loads as her cargo the products of your forests and your fields, and carries them to your markets in our ports in the Orient. The owners of this ship I command operate 50 huge liners in the Oriental trade. Is there two or three or four American companies that combined, operate that many in the same traffic?

"Yet we carry American goods. Why don't you carry your own stuff?

"No, I don't think a ship subsidy will meet the decadent condition of your shipping. The French have such a system, and it has worked incalculable evil. It has sent French ships to destruction, and French seamen to death. The French shipbuilder no longer builds ships for service, but constructs them in the shortest possible time, in order to obtain the government money. Your American shipbuilder may be more honest, but greed is the cardinal sin of America, and I think the experiment might prove disastrous."

Captain Goodwin is the typical ship Master. His face has all the stern, rugged, forceful and genial characteristics that are to be met with in men who have time and again approached close to the death that lurks in disasters at sea – and won out.

After many escapes from adventures that for a time are to be viewed seriously, a man gets to believe in his luck, and that accounts for the geniality.

Over the Coffee and Cigars, Captain Goodwin is apt to grow reminiscent, and after much urging and numerous questions, the conversation will become more personal. He has a fund of stories that voyages of 40 years ago have provided him with, and his accounts of his apprentice days give an intensely vivid picture of the life of the sailor during the last half of the last century.

Captain Goodwin's father was a sailor before him, and his first voyage was from London to New York, which he made with his father in 1861. He was in the latter city during the stirring times of the first departure of troops for the battlefields of the South, and was there when the body of the beloved Captain Ellsworth was returned for burial.

Each trip that Captain Goodwin makes with his ship is a journey of half-way round the world.

# A Survivor Found At Sea

*[Below is a reproduction of a press-cutting, from an unknown newspaper, followed by two statements and a letter, all of which were found among John Goodwin's papers]*

A Thousand Miles From Home

A thrilling story of a four months' drift in the Indian Ocean was recently told by Captain J.H. Goodwin, the master of the steamer Telemachus, which is at present at Port Adelaide. Captain Goodwin, writing to his owners, Messrs. Alfred Holt & Co, stated that on May 7 his ship overhauled a schooner-rigged boat, from which an emaciated man was rescued. There was also in the boat a dead body. This little craft, which was 25 ft. in length, was blown off the Seychelle Islands on January 8, and had been drifting and sailing aimlessly about for four months. The captain said this seemed almost incredible, but in corroboration he enclosed a copy of a statement made by the survivor, and also a letter in French from the owner to the man in charge of the boat. From this statement it appears that the survivor, who was aged 19 years, was third hand on the schooner-rigged boat Sea Queen, owned by his father, a resident of Mahe, Seychelle Islands. In company with the Captain and second hand he sailed from Victoria, Mahe, on January 8, at 10 a.m., for Ause Royale, with a cargo of rice. On the following day, during a mist, they were blown out of their course, as when the weather cleared the islands were no longer visible. For some time they sailed about: then they sighted a Liverpool steamer, from which they received water, potatoes, onions, and some clothes, and were told to steer an east-north-east course. They continued sailing, not knowing their whereabouts, and lost all count of time and dates. Their fresh water ran out, but they collected all they could when it rained, and also caught some fish, which they ate raw. The second hand died of thirst, and his body was put overboard, and the captain died some time before the rescue by the Telemachus: but the survivor states that he had not the strength to put the body overboard. When picked up the boat was 1,000 miles from Mahe, whence it set sail in January.

Captain Goodwin, after reaching home from the trip, was presented by the Lord Mayor in the Liverpool Town Hall with a pair of binoculars, the gift of the Governor and community of the Seychelle Islands, in recognition of his rescue.

We learn from an officer on board the Telemachus that the sailor reached his home safely.

## Statement of J. H. Goodwin

On the 7th day of May 1910 at 2 p.m., weather fine, we sighted a schooner-rigged boat, with sails in rags, and only one man visible. Stopped and got alongside her, found one living emaciated man almost exhausted, got him on board and attended to by Doctor, who reported him to be suffering from privation, hunger, and thirst, and wandering in his mind. Examined the boat and found one naked, dead body of a man lying in the little cuddy. The body was emaciated and decomposing, and the smell very offensive. We found two bags of rice, some stinking raw fish, but not a drop of water and no fuel of any kind.

When we found the boat we were in Lat. 9°.38 N. and Long. 65.34 E. and she had been apparently drifting about for a long time, and all we could get out of the poor creature was 'Mahe, 8th January'. This seemed incredible to me, as we were about N.E. by N. 1,040 miles from Mahe, Seychelle Islands, and could not believe they had been drifting and sailing about for four months, but the accompanying statement by the survivor will show that they were absolutely lost on the wide wide sea for that length of time.

As the boat is to some extent a danger to navigation, and the smell from the corpse very offensive, I had paraffin oil poured over the boat and set her on fire, standing by until she was ablaze fore and aft, and then proceeded on our voyage to Penang.

My name is Josue Green (aged 19). I was third hand on the schooner-rigged boat Sea Queen, owned by my father, William Green of Ause Royale, Mahe, Seychelle Islands.

In company with Athendore Vidot, Captain, and Henry Clothide, second hand, I sailed from the Port of Victoria, Mahe, on the 8th January 1910, at 10 a.m. for Ause Royale, with a cargo of rice, intending to sail from there to L'Hedu Nord, for a cargo of guano for Takamaka, Mahe.

On the 9th January the weather was very bad, heavy rain falling, and it was very misty. This continued until noon, when it cleared up. We then became aware that we had been blown out of our course, and out of sight of the Islands, and our captain did not know where we had got to.

We sailed about for a considerable time, endeavouring to get a sight of land, but could not see any. We however eventually sighted a Liverpool passenger steamer. I saw 'Liverpool' on her stern, but do not know her name. Our Captain went on board, and they gave him some Potatoes, Onions, and a keg of fresh water, and some clothes.

They refused to take us on board, but directed us to steer an E.N.E. course from where we were. We continued sailing, not knowing our whereabouts, and lost all count of time and dates, until all our fresh water was used up. We occasionally had rain, and we collected all we possibly could. We caught some fish, and had to eat it raw. I was reduced to drinking salt water for I think quite a month before I was rescued.

I cannot remember all that happened, or the dates, but Henry Clothide died of thirst before our potatoes were finished, and we put his body overboard. The Captain died some time before I was rescued by the Telemachus, but I had not strength enough to put his body overboard.

I saw two steamers before I was picked up, but evidently they did not notice me, and sailed away. When I saw the Telemachus on the 7th May, I thought she would also pass me, she was going so fast, and I gave up hope, but when I saw her turn and come back I was overjoyed.

The steamer came up alongside me, and a bottle of water was lowered to me, and I had fresh water for the first time for I can not say how many days. This revived me and I was taken aboard the steamer. Our Captain was dead in the boat, and I could stay there no longer, so I remained on the steamer, and my boat after being overhauled by the mate, was destroyed by fire. My boat was 25 feet long, and capable of carrying about four tons of cargo, and traded round the Seychelle Islands.

Everything possible was done for me on the steamer, and I am now feeling much better.

I have written my father to give him the news of my safety, and also the loss of my shipmates and boat. They tell me on board that I was rescued in Lat. 9.38 N. and Long. 65.34 E. - 1,040 miles from Mahe, but how I got there I cannot say.

(Sd) Josue Green

Letter from Josue Green to his father, William Green, Ause Royale, Mahe *[Trans. from French]*

My Dear Father,

I write to you with very good news. Thank God the steamer Telemachus rescued me when I was almost dead. Henry died two or three months ago, but I do not remember the date, but when the steamer rescued me he was there. I had not the strength to remain in the boat, so the sailors took me out and burnt the boat Sea Queen with my permission. This steamer is going to Singapore, and I shall be sent from Singapore to Mahe without anything to pay. It is possible that I shall return via Bombay by a British India Company steamer, or via Suez by a Messageries Maritime steamer. I cannot say when I shall arrive at Mahe, but will let you know as soon as possible. The Captain tells me that when I arrive at Singapore, he will leave me placed in the Sailors' home there, and should you wish to hear further about me, you can write to the Superintendent there, and he will reply to you, letting you know if I have left for Mahe, or where I am to be found.

I am well found on the boat, and the Captain and others treat me as a child of theirs.

Give my compliments to all who you give news to, not forgetting Madame Japhet and little Rose, and all the young ladies, not forgetting Annie and Alfred.

Your devoted son,
*(Sd) Josue Green*